this one goes out to the ones i love...

I dedicate this book to the three most important people in my world: to Drew Potter, most patient husband and fellow dreamer of the dream, thank you for selling me those crimp beads, meeting me for coffee and believing in me even when I couldn't; to my mother, Sharon Scanlin, who showed me that a woman can do and be absolutely anything she can imagine—thank you, Mom, you rock; and finally, to my amazing daughter, Avalon...the world is filled with possibilities and the only limitations are the ones we create, so dream big and break all of the rules!

thank you thank you thank you

To the creative team at North Light and F+W: Karla, Krista, Christine P., Christine D. and Ms. Tricia Waddell, thank you for all of your hard work to help make my first book a reality! To the coolest editor around, Ms. Jessica Gordon, thank you doesn't even begin to cover it, you are the best, are you ready for the next book?! To the Co-Bead Queen of the Universe, Mistress Katie Hacker, thank you for paying it forward. To Vlad, thanks for making me a cool cartoon! To the whole crew at Beadalon, you guys rule! To Kim Paquette...you have made my world a sparkly wonderland! To Iris Johansen (and the late Julia Child), thank you for showing me that it is never too late to reinvent yourself. Special thanks to all of the generous manufacturers, distributors, wholesalers and retailers who provided product to make this book really cool.

table of contents

the impatient BEADER

margot potter

NORTH LIGHT BOOKS

Cincinnati, Ohio
www.artistsnetwork.com

meet the impatient beader

Margot Potter is a woman of many talents...author, designer, actress, vocalist, poet, songwriter, TV personality, thrift
store treasure repurposer and mom to the world's coolest
kid. She resides with her daughter, Avalon; husband,
Drew; a flock of pecky chickens and a snarky, barky terrier
named Mrs. Fellerbee in a 125-year-old former Amish Union
Hall and School House near Lancaster, Pennsylvania. Her
current goal is to become the Bead Queen of the Universe,
and in anticipation of achieving this lofty aspiration she is
busy at work on the world's sparkliest tiara.

© Drew Potter

Published by North Light Books, an imprint of F+W Publications, Inc., 4700
East Galbraith Road, Cincinnati, Ohio 45236. (800) 289-0963. First edition.

10 09 08 07 06   5 4 3 2 1

Distributed in Canada by Fraser Direct
100 Armstrong Avenue
Georgetown, ON, Canada L7G 5S4
Tel: (905) 877-4411
Distributed in the U.K. and Europe by David & Charles
Brunel House, Newton Abbot, Devon, TQ12 4PU, England
Tel: (+44) 1626 323200, Fax: (+44) 1626 323319
Email: mail@davidandcharles.co.uk
Distributed in Australia by Capricorn Link
P.O. Box 704, S. Windsor, NSW 2756 Australia
Tel: (02) 4577-3555

Library of Congress Cataloging-in-Publication Data
Potter, Margot.
  The impatient beader / Margot Potter.
    p. cm.
  Includes index.
  ISBN-13: 978-1-58180-762-2 (alk. paper)
  ISBN-10: 1-58180-762-7
  1. Beadwork. 2. Jewelry making. I. Title.
TT860.P68 2006
745.594'2-dc22
                2005021797

fw
F+W PUBLICATIONS, INC.

EDITOR: Jessica Gordon
DESIGNER: Karla Baker
ILLUSTRATOR: Vladimir Alvarez
LAYOUT ARTIST: Donna Cozatchy
PRODUCTION COORDINATOR: Robin Richie
PHOTOGRAPHERS: Tim Grondin, Al Parrish,
Christine Polomsky, Hal Barkan
PHOTO STYLISTS: Nora Martini, Jan Nickum

METRIC CONVERSION CHART

To convert	to	multiply by
Inches	Centimeters	2.54
Centimeters	Inches	0.4
Feet	Centimeters	30.5
Centimeters	Feet	0.03
Yards	Meters	0.9
Meters	Yards	1.1
Sq. Inches	Sq. Centimeters	6.45
Sq. Centimeters	Sq. Inches	0.16
Sq. Feet	Sq. Meters	0.09
Sq. Meters	Sq. Feet	10.8
Sq. Yards	Sq. Meters	0.8
Sq. Meters	Sq. Yards	1.2
Pounds	Kilograms	0.45
Kilograms	Pounds	2.2
Ounces	Grams	28.3
Grams	Ounces	0.035

get your bead groove on...

There are people who love to spend hours, days, weeks and even months toiling over one project until it is perfectly perfect. These tireless workers are blessed with endless amounts of patience, they are motivated to strive unceasingly to reach their goal, and they revel in the tedium and monotony of endless and repetitive motion. These perfectionists have the most elegant homes, the most fragrant and delicious pies, and the loveliest handcrafted invitations—and to add insult to injury, none of it seems to make them sweat.

If you are one of these people, this book is not for you.

If instead you are a creative individual who lacks time, focus or motivation, you have come to the right place. Greetings and welcome to the wonderful world of beading for the patience impaired.

As I began to work on this book, I realized just how impatient I am—and I mean this seriously. I am impatient. It takes a very concerted effort for me to meticulously finish just about anything. Every scarf I attempt to knit becomes a lovely potholder. Every present I wrap is beautiful on top and a tape disaster underneath. I am particularly happy

when my efforts are rewarded with maximum success for minimum effort. This is why I love beadwork.

Now don't let me steer you wrong. Beadwork is hardly all fun and games. I had to spend a fair amount of time problem solving to create the designs in this book—each design represents hours of testing the limitations and the potential of the materials. I love the challenge that beadwork presents, and I hope you will too. Once you master the basic techniques, the level of time and energy you will need to commit to making designs is completely up to you. It isn't rocket science, as they say, and in my humble opinion some of the most wonderful designs are the most simple. The best thing about beadwork is that you can have a finished product to proudly wear, gift or display in a relatively short amount of time. You can't wear your scrapbook now, can you?!

I have laid the foundation here for you to become a beading whiz. I've supplied you with a plethora of techniques and design ideas for your beading enjoyment. I have created fun and rewarding step-by-step designs for you to follow, or you may strike out on your own with these ideas to serve as your road map. Within an hour or two, you will have a finished piece of wearable art—how is that for almost instant gratification? Now grab some beads and let's get started.

SKILL LEVEL GUIDE:

To make things easy for you, I've assigned each project in the book a skill level—that way you'll know which projects I consider really easy and which ones I think might be a little tougher for someone just starting out. Following is a key that explains the three skill levels:

If you're a **BEADING VIRGIN**, you'll find the simple stringing projects the easiest.

If you're a **BEADING VIXEN**, you're ready to step it up a little and try something a bit more challenging—maybe something with dangles or linked chain.

If you're a **BEADING GODDESS**, well, then you can do anything you want. If you want a challenge, these projects are for you.

tools, materials + findings, oh my!

To execute the designs in this book, you'll need to acquire the proper findings, tools and stringing materials. Then you'll need to master just a few (very easy) basic techniques. Getting through these beginning stages might require some practice and a pinch of patience, but both will be minimal. I know, this is supposed to be a book for the impatient—but you can do it, I promise!

BEADING TOOLS

My most valuable beading advice is to buy the proper tools. When I started getting into beadwork, I used a broken pair of needle-nose carpentry pliers for about two years. I would finish off a design and my pliers would cut the wire, sending beads flying in all directions. I didn't know any better, but since you are reading this book, you have no excuses! You can find good beading tools at your local bead retailer, in catalogs and online. You don't need the super-deluxe-fancy-schmancy tools to get started, but you do need tools designed specifically for beading. The new ergonomic tools are excellent for people with dexterity issues or carpal tunnel syndrome, and using them now will help you avoid developing either! If you get really serious, you may wish to upgrade to professional quality tools. Below you'll find a list of what you will need (the essentials have a star).

MIGHTY CRIMP TOOL

MICRO CRIMP TOOL

REGULAR CRIMP TOOL

NEEDLE- or **CHAIN-NOSE PLIERS** have long, pointed jaws and are a must-have in any jeweler's beading box. Use them to tuck, secure, pull, grasp and turn wire.

SNIPE- and **SHORT SNIPE-NOSE PLIERS** are top-of-the-line pointed-nose pliers. With their finer pincers, they are particularly effective for working with smaller diameters of sterling wire. The smaller tip allows you to work easily in tight spaces. If you don't want to splurge for these pliers right away, just substitute needle- or chain-nose pliers wherever snipe- and short snipe-nose pliers are listed.

ROUND-NOSE PLIERS have rounded cone-shaped jaws that are used to shape and form wire for looped and coiled earrings, dangles and charms. They are another must-have item.

BEST SNIPE-NOSE PLIERS

BEST SHORT SNIPE-NOSE PLIERS

BEST ROUND-NOSE PLIERS

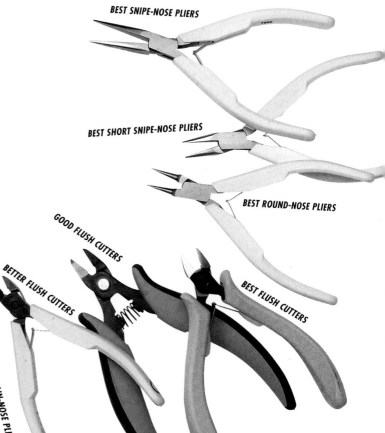

GOOD CHAIN-NOSE PLIERS

GOOD ROUND-NOSE PLIERS

GOOD NEEDLE-NOSE PLIERS

BETTER ROUND-NOSE PLIERS

BETTER CHAIN-NOSE PLIERS

BETTER FLUSH CUTTERS

GOOD FLUSH CUTTERS

BEST FLUSH CUTTERS

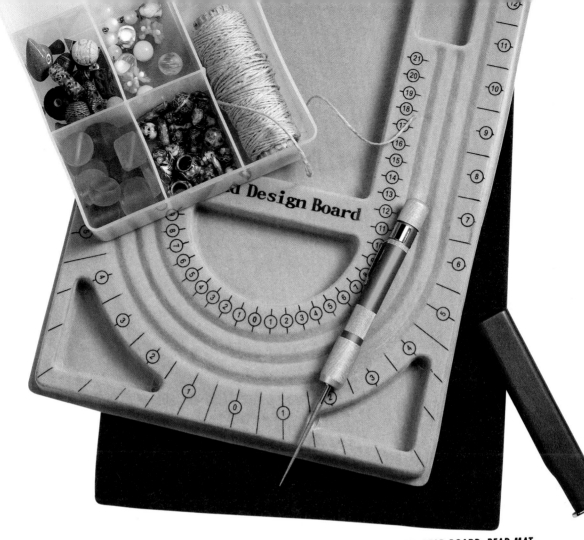

FROM LEFT TO RIGHT: BEAD BOX, BEAD BOARD, BEAD MAT (BOTTOM), HAND BEAD REAMER, TRI-CORD KNOTTER

A **CRIMP TOOL** is used to round and secure crimp beads and tubes to prevent any sharp edges that can cut your wires and your skin, giving your jewelry a professional finish. (Try the micro crimp tool for small crimp tubes and wire and the mighty size for leather, cording and large-diameter wire.)

FLUSH CUTTERS are wire cutters designed to snip beading wire and metal to create a flush cut for a finished design. When you've been beading for a while, reward yourself by upgrading to an ergonomic flush cutter.

OBLIQUE CUTTERS are angled precision wire cutters that have a finer tip to allow you to get in closer when cutting wires and pins. If you haven't quite worked your way up to oblique cutters, flush cutters will work just fine wherever these cutters are listed.

A **BEAD BOARD** is an incredibly helpful and versatile tool that no designer should be without. A bead board measures your design, keeps your beads from running away and gives you a preview of the finished look before you commit.

A **BEAD MAT** is an excellent no-slip surface for laying out seed beads or small beads that are impossible to design with on the bead board. It keeps those little beads from escaping.

BEAD BOXES are inexpensive plastic tackle box-style trays that work perfectly as storage containers for beads. You can arrange your beads by color or style and have them at the ready when you are.

A **WOODEN BEAD CADDY** keeps your tools, strands and materials organized and within arm's reach.

A **BEAD REAMER** is a tool with an attachment like a drill bit used to smooth the rough edges on glass or gemstone beads before you string to keep the wires and strand from wearing easily. A bead reamer can also be worked back and forth inside a bead's hole to widen the hole and expand the options for stringing materials. A hand reamer is an affordable option for the beginner, but if you decide to up the ante, the electric reamer makes your work fast and easy.

The **TRI-CORD KNOTTER** is a patented three-pronged bead-knotting tool that saves much time and effort in creating knots between beads. You can opt to use an awl and your hands, but the Tri-Cord Knotter makes knotting far easier.

MATERIALS

After you've collected the requisite tools (begged, borrowed or bought...), the next step is to purchase beading materials. I highly recommend using good beading materials—it turns out to be a patience booster: When you use good materials you achieve good results, just like using fresh, top-quality ingredients makes a good meal. You also avoid having to rework a broken design. A word of warning: Do not bead with dental floss or plastic fishing line. Dental floss is terrific for flossing teeth and fishing line is excellent for catching fish. Please use wire and strand specifically designed for beadwork—you can thank me later. You'll find these materials at bead retailers, in catalogs and online.

CABLED MULTISTRAND BEADING WIRE is comprised of multiple strands of stainless steel wire cabled and coated with nylon. Cabled beading wire comes in multiple strand counts—the higher the strand count, the stronger and more supple the wire. In the supplies lists for the projects, I list multiple strand counts to give you options. While it's always better to use the higher strand count, the lower strand counts work fine as well, and the wire is more economically priced. The strands are measured in width starting with the thinnest at .010" (.25mm) and moving up. The larger the number, the thicker the wire. Try to fill the holes of your beads with the wire to prevent early wear. See the packaging for the manufacturer's recommendations. I recommend this type of wire for most of your stringing projects.

COLORED COPPER WIRE comes in many, many colors including silver- and gold-plated, and also in a wide range of gauges (a.k.a. diameters). If you find that you enjoy wire work, you can also purchase sterling silver and gold-filled wire.

MEMORY WIRE is a preformed steel wire that stays permanently in a rounded shape. It is available in gold- and silver-tone and comes in ring, bracelet and necklace sizes.

LEATHER CORDING and **SUEDE LACING** are an alternative to bead wire, and work well for beads with larger holes.

SILK or **NYLON BEAD THREAD** is used primarily for knotted designs. Thread comes in a wide variety of colors and sizes, so make sure you get the right size for the beads you use or your bead holes will eat your knots.

INSIDE WOODEN BEAD CADDY: FLUSH CUTTERS, COLORED CABLED MULTISTRAND BEADING WIRE, COLORED COPPER WIRE, DYED HEMP

LEATHER CORDING

STRETCH CORDING

BEAD THREAD

LINKED CHAIN

SILVER MEMORY WIRE

STRETCH CORDING comes in two varieties that work well for stretch designs. Flat fibrous nylon material comes in several colors and diameters and is excellent for stringing crystals, seed beads and gemstones—it is very supple and easy to weave. Monofilament transparent stretch cording also comes in a wide palette of colors and a wide variety of diameters, and is particularly good for single-strand or power bracelet designs. Fabric-coated rubber band cording can break and wears very easily.

HEMP CORD is a strong natural fiber—the world's longest and strongest—that works best with beads that have larger holes. It comes in many colors and diameters and makes lovely knotted jewelry. Contrary to prevalent beliefs, you absolutely can't get a buzz from smoking hemp, so it would probably be better to use it in your beading! If you are a fan of conspiracy theories, read up on the smear campaign that was created by DuPont and Hearst to discredit hemp in the 1930s.

PREMADE CHAIN is available in base and precious metal and comes in many styles, sizes and finishes. It's an amazing time-saver for the designer and gives even simple designs an edge.

FINDINGS

Findings are components (in addition to beads and stringing materials) used to make jewelry. Clasps, earring parts and spacer bars are all findings. They can be simple and functional or they can become part of the overall design. Findings come in base metal and precious metal and in various finishes, sizes and diameters (gauges). Jump rings, head pins, eye pins, crimp tubes and some other findings come in packets—each packet may include anywhere from a few (4 or 5) to lots (100+). One packet of head pins, for example, may contain plenty for several projects.

JUMP RINGS are metal rings used to create dangles, chains and connectors.

HEAD PINS are metal pins with a flat bottom, or head, to secure beads when creating dangles. Use the gauge that is appropriate for the size of the holes in your beads. (Smaller bead holes require higher gauges.)

EYE PINS are similar to head pins, but they have a rounded loop on one end for making beaded chains and multiple-dangle earrings.

CRIMP BEADS and tubes are tiny metal beads and tubes used to secure wire to clasps. Beads and tubes function identically, but tubes create a more finished appearance.

FOLD-OVER ENDS are metal components used with leather, suede and cording to create a clean way to attach a clasp. Bend the metal flaps around the ends of the cording with chain-nose pliers.

CLAMSHELLS AND TIPS are small metal components used to cover end knots in knotted designs. The shell folds over to conceal the knot within, "swallowing" it.

SPACER BARS are flat bars with multiple holes used in multi-strand designs to create proper spacing.

LANYARDS are large clasps used for badges and IDs.

A **LOBSTER CLASP** looks like a lobster claw and is tremendously versatile.

A **HOOK AND EYE CLASP** is a fish-hook style end that secures into a figure eight component. Tighten with your pliers to secure it, if necessary.

A **FILIGREE LOCKING CLASP** is a fancy clasp that locks closed securely, and is great for maximum security.

MULTISTRAND CLASPS are used when stringing more than one strand to give the design proper spacing. They are available in multiple sizes, shapes and numbers of loops.

TOGGLE CLASPS have two components: a circle (or other open shape) and toggle bar which threads through the open shape. They are often beautifully embellished and can become an integral part of the design of any piece.

FROM LEFT TO RIGHT, BOTTOM TO TOP: CLAMSHELLS AND TIPS, CLASPS (SEE DESCRIPTIONS ABOVE), DECORATIVE HEAD PINS, HEAD PINS, EYE PINS, JUMP RINGS, FOLD-OVER ENDS, SPACER BARS, CRIMP TUBES AND BEADS, EARRING FINDINGS

beads, beads, wonderful beads

I love beads. I really, really love them. There is something thrilling about going to a bead show, bead store or bead warehouse and picking through strands of pearls, Czech glass, Austrian crystal, semiprecious gemstones, metal, plastic…I get excited just writing about it. There are literally millions of beads out there and every style invites the designer to create. If you are at all creative, you will find that beads will lead you if you let them. Gather up a pleasing array of beads and then play. I keep my beads in sectioned trays on angled shelving so that I can see the entire selection at all times. I spend hours juxtaposing beads against one another, looking for new and exciting combinations. Be creative in finding your beads—I chance across wonderful beads in old costume jewelry at thrift shops and flea markets. Take old jewelry apart and repurpose it. Think of it as freeing the beads! Combine the old with the new—make surprising choices in color, texture and combination.

BEAD LINGO

AB: aurora borealis (oil slick) finish on crystal and glass beads

FACETED: precision cuts made in the bead material to refract light and create sparkle

FIRE-POLISHED: the finish on faceted glass beads that have been reheated to soften the faceted edges

SP: silver-plated metal or plastic

HANK: multiple strands of the same bead style bundled together, mainly used in wholesale situations

STRAND: beads come on temporary strands; it's cheaper to buy them on the strand than individually

BICONE: a bead that looks like two cones connected at their bases

RONDELLE A.K.A. DONUT: a bead shaped like a donut with a small center hole

SPACER: usually a metal bead used to accent a design

BRIOLETTE: a teardrop-shaped bead that is faceted from every angle

TEARDROP: similar to the briolette, but longer and leaner

CHICLET OR PUFFY SQUARE: puffed and rounded square bead

RICE PEARL: teeny tiny freshwater pearls shaped like rice

COIN PEARL: a flat coin-shaped freshwater cultured pearl

INSIDE COLOR: clear beads with a colored center

CHANNEL: a flat bead framed in metal

CRYSTAL: leaded glass material used to create super sparkly beads (this can also refer to a gemstone material)

BEAD SIZING

Beads are measured in millimeters—it's the metric system, remember it?

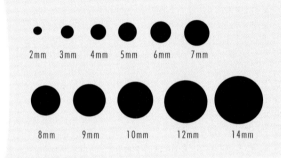

2mm 3mm 4mm 5mm 6mm 7mm

8mm 9mm 10mm 12mm 14mm

STANDARD NECKLACE LENGTHS

16" (41CM) CHOKER

18" (46CM) PRINCESS

24" (61CM) MATINEE

32" (81CM) OPERA

48" (122CM) ROPE

NOTE: To make a fitted choker 15" (38cm) or smaller, you will need to measure your neck for your own specific fit.

DESIGNER TIP

When buying beads, here is the general guideline for how many to buy to make a 16" (41cm) finished necklace length:

2mm ≈ 200 beads
3mm ≈ 135 beads
4mm ≈ 100 beads
6mm ≈ 68 beads
8mm ≈ 50 beads
10mm ≈ 25 beads

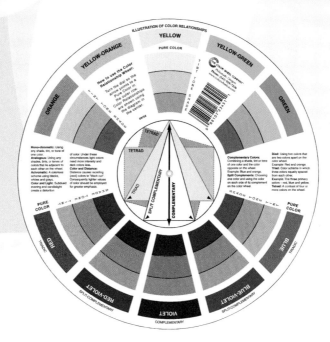

DESIGNER TIP: COLOR WHEEL

Every girl needs a color wheel to help decipher the language of color. Complementary, analogous, split complementary…If these terms aren't familiar, a color wheel makes it easy for you to brush up on the color basics. It's a very useful tool—so pick one up!

BEAD STYLES

Beads come in virtually any material you can imagine. In addition to the beads listed below, look for cloisonné, porcelain, clay, polymer clay, bone, wood, straw, nut…every culture has its own unique beads. Become a bead explorer!

VINTAGE GLASS and **PLASTIC BEADS:** Beautiful vintage German and Czech glass beads can be found at bead shows and in old costume jewelry. Lucite and plastic beads from the 1940s–1970s add a retro vibe.

ANTIQUE GLASS BEADS (African, Venetian, Dutch, etc.)**:** These "GOBs," or Good Old Beads, can be centuries old. Used in ancient trade routes, they are often sold as "African" beads, but many originated in Venice and Holland. Mali wedding beads (the flat teardrop and light bulb shapes) are made in Mali and are traditionally worn by brides. Be careful when buying "old" beads, as there are plenty of fakes on the market.

SEED BEADS: The best seed beads come from Japan, then the Czech Republic, then China and then India. If you are weaving, the more consistent the size of your beads, the more consistent your finished design.

SWAROVSKI CRYSTAL: In my opinion, this is the finest crystal on Earth. Made in Austria to exacting standards, no other crystal beads compare for color and sparkle—look out for "knockovski" fake crystals.

CZECH GLASS: Whimsical, beautiful and wondrous in their seemingly endless variety, Czech glass beads are a delight! The Czech people are glass bead masters and have been making these beads for generations.

CHINESE GLASS: The Chinese are innovators, but also masters at faking it. Far more affordable than the glass beads and gemstones they mimic, they offer the financially challenged more options. Look for affordable lamp-worked and striated styles, new to the market.

GEMSTONES, PEARLS and **SHELL BEADS:** Beautiful beads crafted from semiprecious gemstones in an amazing array of styles, shapes and materials have flooded the bead market recently. Take advantage of this bead boom and stock up! Freshwater pearls from China are available in beautiful colors and shapes at reasonable prices. Most of the colors are dyed or irradiated, so check for color fastness before you buy!

INDIAN GLASS BEADS: Caned and lamp-worked handmade glass beads from India are surprisingly affordable and wonderfully fun for the bead artist.

METAL BEADS, SPACERS, CHARMS and **SLIDERS:** Look for plated metal beads to add a little spice to your designs. Many newer styles mimic Southeast Asian silverwork.

STERLING- and **GOLD-FILLED:** Thai and Balinese silver artisans have perfected handmade silverwork to make lovely oxidized textured beads. Sterling- and gold-filled beads are more expensive, but make for professional-looking jewelry.

VINTAGE GLASS AND PLASTIC BEADS

SILVER BALI BEADS

SEED BEADS

CZECH GLASS BEADS

METAL CHARMS

CAT'S EYE GLASS BEADS

STERLING- AND GOLD-FILLED BEADS

SEMIPRECIOUS GEMSTONE BEADS

PEARLS AND SHELL BEADS

ANTIQUE GLASS BEADS

STRAND OF INDIAN GLASS BEADS

SWAROVSKI CRYSTALS

bead basics

ATTACHING A CRIMP TUBE

This is one of the easiest and most secure methods for attaching a clasp to a wire. I highly recommend you use this method to give your jewelry a finished and professional look.

SLIDE CRIMP TUBE ONTO WIRE

CUT A LENGTH OF WIRE ABOUT 4" (10CM) LONGER THAN THE FINISHED LENGTH OF THE PIECE. THREAD A CRIMP TUBE ONTO ONE END OF THE WIRE, ABOUT 2" (5CM) FROM THE END.

PATIENCE BOOSTER

Don't allow the wires to cross in the crimp tube, even though they want to cross naturally. They should be side by side for the crimping to work properly.

SLIDE WIRE BACK THROUGH CRIMP TUBE

THREAD THE END OF THE WIRE THROUGH THE CLASP AND BACK THROUGH THE CRIMP TUBE, ALLOWING A LITTLE OF THE END OF THE WIRE TO STICK THROUGH THE CRIMP TUBE. SLIDE THE CRIMP TUBE UP ON THE WIRE, LEAVING ABOUT ⅛" (3MM) BETWEEN THE CLASP AND THE TUBE TO PREVENT RAPID WEAR ON THE WIRE.

FLATTEN CRIMP TUBE

PLACE THE CRIMP TUBE IN THE FIRST INDENTATION OF THE CRIMP TOOL. CLOSE THE JAWS OF THE CRIMP TOOL AND MASH THE CRIMP TUBE, SMASHING IT AND CRIMPING IT FLAT. THERE WILL BE AN INDENTATION ON ONE SIDE OF THE CRIMP TUBE AND THE OTHER SIDE WILL BE CURVED AND SMOOTH.

CHECK TO MAKE SURE WIRES ARE STRAIGHT

AFTER CRIMPING THE TUBE, EACH WIRE SHOULD BE NEATLY SEPARATED BY THE METAL TUBE, NOT CROSSING.

FOLD CRIMP TUBE IN HALF

PLACE THE CRIMPED TUBE VERTICALLY INTO THE FIRST
SLOT ON THE CRIMP TOOL WITH THE SMOOTH SIDE
FACING TOWARD THE JAWS OF THE PLIERS AND FOLD
THE TUBE IN HALF.

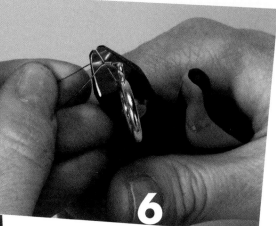

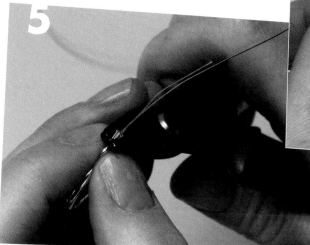

TRIM END OF WIRE

USE FLUSH CUTTERS TO TRIM THE EXCESS TAIL
OF THE WIRE, MAKING SURE TO CUT THE
WIRE FLUSH AGAINST THE CRIMP TUBE.

OPENING + CLOSING A JUMP RING

When secured properly, jump rings provide an easy way to attach dangles and charms
to your jewelry. Always double-check to be certain the jump ring is completely closed
with tension to prevent losing your dangles!

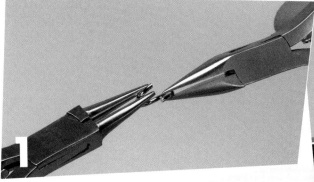

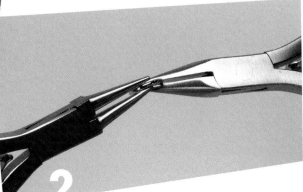

OPEN JUMP RING

FIND THE BREAK IN THE WIRE JUMP RING AND GRAB ONTO THE
WIRE ON EACH SIDE OF THE BREAK WITH A PAIR OF PLIERS. OPEN
THE JUMP RING BY MOVING THE ENDS IN OPPOSITE DIRECTIONS,
ONE TOWARD YOU AND ONE AWAY FROM YOU. DON'T OPEN
THEM BY PULLING THE ENDS AWAY FROM EACH OTHER BECAUSE
IT WILL DISTORT THE JUMP RING.

CLOSE JUMP RING

CLOSE THE JUMP RING THE SAME WAY, BY MOVING
THE ENDS OF THE JUMP RING BACK TOWARD EACH
OTHER. APPLY PRESSURE WHILE MOVING TO WORK
THE OPENING SECURELY CLOSED.

TURNING A HEAD PIN

The turned or looped head pin is an essential skill for making earrings, charms and dangles. Practice makes perfect here—as you master the technique, your loops will continue to improve.

BEND WIRE

SLIDE THE BEAD ONTO A HEAD PIN AND BEND THE REMAINDER OF THE WIRE WITH YOUR FINGERS AT A 90° ANGLE, FLUSH TO THE TOP OF THE BEAD.

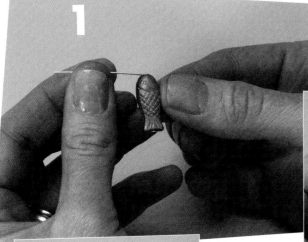

BEGIN TO MAKE LOOP

USE ROUND-NOSE PLIERS AND GRAB THE WIRE DIRECTLY AFTER THE BEND AND TURN THE PLIERS TOWARD YOURSELF. POSITIONING THE WIRE TOWARD THE TIPS OF THE PLIERS MAKES THE LOOPS FINER AND SMOOTHER.

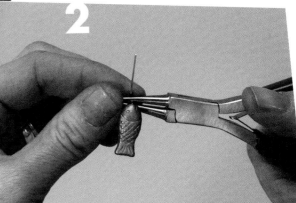

CREATE LOOP IN WIRE

USE YOUR FINGERS TO TWIST THE WIRE AROUND THE PLIERS TO FORM A COMPLETE LOOP. WITH PRACTICE, YOU WILL GET A FEEL FOR THIS.

CLIP WIRE TAIL

CLIP THE WIRE TAIL WITH THE FLUSH CUTTERS TO CREATE A FLUSH LOOP. THE FLAT END OF THE CUTTERS SHOULD BE FACING UP, THUS CREATING A FLUSH CUT. (IF THE TIP OF THE WIRE IS POINTED, IT IS NOT FLUSH CUT.)

TIGHTEN LOOP

USE CHAIN-NOSE PLIERS TO TIGHTEN THE LOOP SO THAT IT IS FULLY CLOSED WITH NO GAPS.

MAKING A WRAPPED (COILED) HEAD PIN LOOP

The wrapped or coiled head pin is another essential skill for making earrings and dangles. This method creates a secure finish and can also become a decorative aspect of your design.

GRAB WIRE ON OTHER SIDE OF BEND
MOVE THE PLIERS SLIGHTLY AROUND THE BEND SO THAT THEY ARE POSITIONED AFTER THE BEND IN THE WIRE.

BEND WIRE
SLIDE THE BEAD ONTO A HEAD PIN AND GRAB THE WIRE DIRECTLY ABOVE THE BEAD WITH THE ROUND-NOSE PLIERS. BEND THE WIRE WITH YOUR FINGERS TO A 90° ANGLE, JUST AS WHEN TURNING A HEAD PIN.

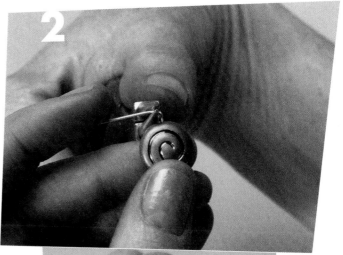

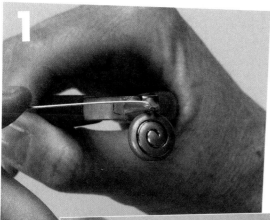

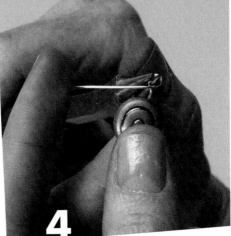

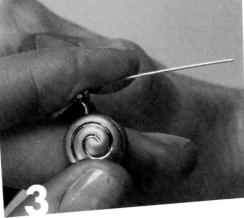

BEGIN TO CREATE LOOP
USE YOUR FINGERS TO BEND THE WIRE UP AND OVER THE NOSE OF THE PLIERS AND SIMULTANEOUSLY MOVE THE PLIERS TOWARD YOU TO START MAKING A LOOP.

PREPARE TO CREATE COIL
CONTINUE HOLDING THE LOOP YOU MADE WITH THE ROUND-NOSE PLIERS AND HOLD THE BEAD BETWEEN YOUR THUMB AND MIDDLE FINGER. BEGIN TO PUSH ON THE TAIL OF THE WIRE WITH YOUR INDEX FINGER.

BEGIN TO CREATE COIL

CONTINUE TO HOLD ON TO THE LOOP WITH THE ROUND-NOSE PLIERS. BEGIN TO WRAP THE TAIL OF THE WIRE AROUND THE BASE OF THE LOOP BY PUSHING IT WITH YOUR INDEX FINGER. IF USING A BASE METAL HEAD PIN, YOU MAY HAVE TO USE ANOTHER PAIR OF PLIERS TO WRAP THE STIFFER METAL.

FINISH WRAPPING LOOP

CONTINUE TO WRAP THE WIRE AROUND THE BASE OF THE LOOP TWO TO THREE TIMES UNTIL THE WRAPPED WIRE IS FLUSH WITH THE TOP OF THE BEAD. DON'T CREATE TOO MUCH PRESSURE AGAINST THE TOP OF THE BEAD BECAUSE GLASS OR GEMSTONE BEADS CAN CRACK OR CHIP.

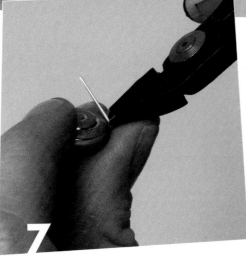

CUT EXCESS WIRE

CUT OFF THE WIRE TAIL WITH FLUSH CUTTERS, AGAIN WITH THE FLAT SIDE FACING AWAY FROM THE TAIL END TO MAKE A FLUSH CUT.

TIGHTEN WRAP

TUCK THE VERY END OF THE WIRE TAIL INTO THE WRAP BY TIGHTENING IT WITH THE CHAIN-NOSE PLIERS.

MAKING YOUR OWN JUMP RINGS

It's easy to create your own jump rings, and it's a useful skill to have. Sometimes when working with colored wire, you may want jump rings to coordinate, or you might run out of or need a specific size of jump ring.

CUT JUMP RINGS

SLIDE THE COILED WIRE OFF OF THE DOWEL ROD AND USE YOUR WIRE CUTTERS TO CUT THE COIL INTO JUMP RINGS, BEING CAREFUL TO KEEP THE WIRE TIGHTLY COILED (STRETCHING THE COIL OUT WILL DISTORT THE ROUND SHAPE OF THE JUMP RINGS).

COIL WIRE AROUND DOWEL

FIND A DOWEL ROD OR A SLIM WOODEN STAKE THAT IS THE DIAMETER YOU WOULD LIKE FOR YOUR JUMP RINGS AND COIL THE WIRE AROUND IT. EACH WRAP MAKES ONE JUMP RING.

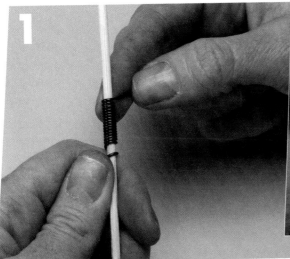

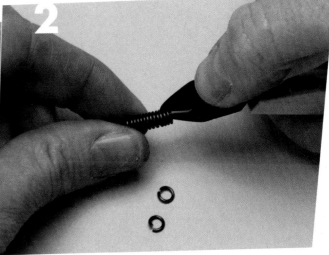

SAY HELLO TO YOUR FRIEND, *THE BEAD BOARD*

Here is some really important advice: Take the time to arrange your beads on a bead board before you string. This is particularly important for the patience factor. It is far easier to change your pattern before you string than it is to take a finished design apart and start over. The bead board will give you measurement and an overview of the final effect. If you will take a moment to look at the board, you will see that it has numbers on it—these are measurements in inches (half and whole). When you build your design up to the same number on each side, you double this number to determine the finished length (don't forget to include your clasp here). For example, if you build up to 8" (20cm) on each side, you will have a 16" (41cm) finished necklace. Please believe me when I tell you that the bead board is your friend! I spend hours at my bead board moving the beads around until I am pleased with the design. Nothing will make you want to give up on beadwork more quickly than restringing unappealing designs.

baby steps

YOU HAVE TO START SOMEWHERE, AND THE BEGINNING IS A VERY GOOD PLACE TO START. MASTER THIS CHAPTER AND YOU WILL BE WELL ON YOUR WAY TO BECOMING A BEAD DIVA. DID YOU PRACTICE USING YOUR CRIMP TOOL? READY, SET, BEAD!

In this chapter, you will learn the most basic jewelry-making techniques and design concepts. It is very important before getting started that you practice attaching a clasp to a wire with a crimp tube. If you wish to make the coordinating earrings, you will also need to practice creating coiled and turned head pin loops. If you never learn anything more than how to string beads on nylon-coated bead wire and how to make simple drop earrings, you will have all of the skills you need to make lovely jewelry for years to come. As you work these single-strand designs, consider playing with the colors, shapes and textures of the beads you choose. Altering the design of these simpler pieces will help you to feel more comfortable branching out and playing with the design of more complicated, multistrand pieces.

"WHEN CHOOSING BETWEEN TWO EVILS I LIKE TO TRY THE ONE I'VE NEVER TRIED BEFORE."
—MAE WEST

TECHNIQUES

- **WORKING WITH THE BEAD BOARD**
- **STRINGING A PREDETERMINED DESIGN**
- **ATTACHING A CLASP**
- **CREATING A LARIAT (NO-CLASP LOOK)**
- **MAKING A BEAD-EMBELLISHED PENDANT**

PALM BEACH
NECKLACE

**TAKING ITS COLOR CUES
FROM THE BOLD CITRUS HUES
OF 1960s RESORT WEAR,**
this necklace is the perfect complement
to an A-line retro print dress. Add a
funky straw hat, sassy sandals and a
ladylike straw bag and you'll feel like
you're at the beach wherever you go!
This is my homage to the stylish Lovey
Howell of *Gilligan's Island* fame.

**5MM CHARTREUSE GREEN
AB CZECH RONDELLE**

**SIZE 15 GREEN
SEED BEAD**

**10MM X 14MM ORANGE STRIATED
CZECH GLASS WINDOWPANE BEAD**

**10MM X 12MM SAGE GREEN
FLAT RECTANGLE BEAD**

8MM LIME LUCITE BEAD

**LARGE STERLING
RONDELLE**

WHAT YOU WILL NEED

SUPPLIES
❋ **7** 10mm x 14mm orange striated Czech glass windowpane beads
❋ **12** 10mm x 12mm sage green flat rectangle beads
❋ **6** 10mm round chartreuse Cat's Eye or 8mm vintage lime Lucite beads
❋ **12** large sterling rondelles
❋ **1** tube size 15 green seed beads
❋ **14** 5mm chartreuse green AB Czech rondelle beads
❋ sterling hook and eye clasp
❋ **2** no. 2 crimp tubes
❋ 20" (51cm) .013" (.33mm) 49 strand wire

TOOLS
❋ crimp tool
❋ flush cutters
❋ bead board

RESOURCES: CZECH GLASS AND RECTANGLES FROM YORK
NOVELTY; LUCITE FROM THE BEADIN' PATH OR CAT'S EYE FROM
BEADALON; STERLING SILVER FINDINGS FROM MARVIN
SCHWAB; WIRE FROM BEADALON

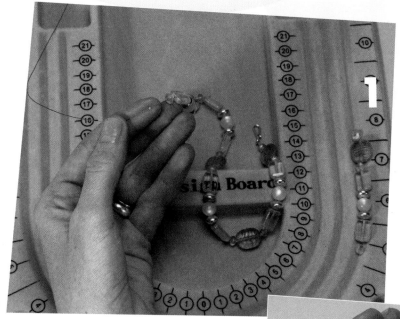

1 ATTACH CLASP AND STRING BEADS

LAY OUT ALL OF THE BEADS ON THE BEAD BOARD IN THE PATTERN AS SHOWN IN THE DIAGRAM, BEGINNING WITH A GREEN SEED BEAD. ATTACH ONE END OF THE CLASP TO THE BEADING WIRE WITH A CRIMP TUBE (SEE TECHNIQUES, PAGE 14). STRING THE BEADS ONTO THE WIRE, ADDING A SEED BEAD BETWEEN ALL OF THE BEADS EXCEPT BETWEEN THE STERLING RONDELLES. (THE LARGE HOLES IN THE RONDELLES SWALLOW UP TINY SEED BEADS.)

PATIENCE BOOSTER

By using tiny seed beads as spacers between larger beads, you get a beautiful drape similar to hand knotting…without actually having to knot…a perfect cheater for the patience impaired.

2 FINISH NECKLACE

FINISH STRINGING THE BEADS ONTO THE WIRE AND ATTACH THE OTHER END OF THE CLASP TO THE END OF THE WIRE, AGAIN USING A CRIMP TUBE. CUT OFF THE EXCESS WIRE WITH FLUSH CUTTERS.

quickie: PALM BEACH EARRINGS

To create a matching pair of earrings, bead a head pin with an orange windowpane bead and a Lucite round bead. Coil the head pin and attach it to a doublelooped eye pin strung with a green rondelle. Add the dangle to a French ear wire using your pliers to secure it (see Techniques, starting on page 14). Repeat to make the matching earring. *Voilá*, you have a sassy set of earrings, just like that!

SURF BETTY
ANKLET

FUN AND FLIRTY FLIP-FLOP ANKLETS ARE THE PERFECT ACCESSORIES FOR HOT SUMMER BEACH DAYS.
Whip up a few of these in a matter of minutes, apply sunscreen, grab your boogie board and shimmy on down the boardwalk in style. From the top of your straw hat to the tips of your painted toes, accessorizing is as much a part of fun at the beach as the sun and sand.

WHAT YOU WILL NEED

SUPPLIES
* pink flip-flop charm
* approx. **72** 3mm light rose AB crystals
* SP filigree box clasp
* **2** no. 2 SP crimp tubes
* approx. 12" (30cm) .018" (.46mm) 7 or 19 strand wire

TOOLS
* crimp tool
* flush cutters
* bead board
* measuring tape

RESOURCES: FLIP-FLOP CHARMS FROM HIRSCHBERG SCHUTZ; CRYSTALS FROM SWAROVSKI; SEED BEADS FROM BLUE MOON BEADS; WIRE AND CLASPS FROM BEADALON

LAY OUT BEADS ON BEAD BOARD

MEASURE YOUR ANKLE, MAKING SURE TO INCLUDE THE LENGTH OF THE CLASP IN YOUR MEASUREMENT. (MY ANKLET IS ABOUT 10" [25CM] LONG.) THEN LAY OUT YOUR CRYSTALS AND YOUR CLASP ON THE BEAD BOARD UNTIL YOU REACH THE APPROPRIATE LENGTH. (YOU MAY ADD OR DELETE BEADS BASED ON YOUR DESIRED FINISHED LENGTH.)

ATTACH ONE END OF CLASP

ATTACH ONE END OF THE CLASP BY STRINGING A CRIMP TUBE AND THE CLASP ONTO A 12" (30CM) LENGTH OF WIRE (FINISHED LENGTH PLUS 2" [5CM]). THREAD THE WIRE BACK THROUGH THE CRIMP TUBE AND FLATTEN THE TUBE WITH THE CRIMP TOOL, THEN FOLD THE FLATTENED TUBE IN HALF WITH THE CRIMP TOOL. CUT OFF THE END OF THE SHORT WIRE WITH FLUSH CUTTERS (SEE TECHNIQUES, PAGE 14).

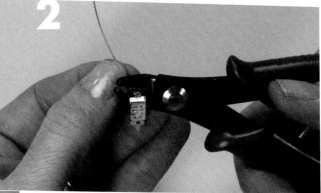

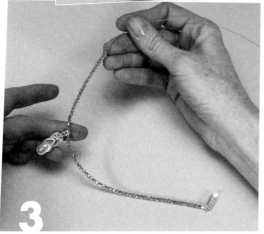

BEAD ANKLET

BEGIN STRINGING THE CRYSTALS ONTO THE WIRE ONE BY ONE. WHEN YOU HAVE STRUNG ON HALF OF THE CRYSTALS, SLIDE ON A FLIP-FLOP CHARM. CONTINUE BEADING THE OTHER HALF OF THE ANKLET.

FINISH ANKLET

WHEN ALL OF THE CRYSTALS ARE IN PLACE, ATTACH THE OTHER END OF THE CLASP. MAKE SURE THAT YOUR CLASP IS CLOSED WHEN YOU CRIMP THE OTHER END OF THE CLASP ON SO THAT THERE IS ENOUGH PLAY IN THE WIRE. IF YOU DO NOT ROUND THE WIRE BEFORE YOU ATTACH THE FINAL CRIMP TUBE, THE DESIGN WILL BE TOO STIFF. ROUNDING THE WIRE ALLOWS ENOUGH SPACE—OR "PLAY"—BETWEEN THE BEADS SO THAT IT WILL DRAPE NICELY WHEN WORN. TO FINISH, FLUSH CUT THE END OF THE WIRE.

quickie: ANKLETS IN OTHER COLORS

Once you've made one anklet, you may just find that you can't stop there. Make as many bright little anklets as you like using any charms or small beads that strike your fancy. One good rule of thumb is to keep the anklets light for a comfortable finished design—unless you're on house arrest, a giant ankle bracelet is entirely uncalled for!

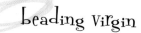

AMAZON WARRIOR
CHOKER

IN THIS BOLD AND EXOTIC DESIGN, COOL COLORS AND A VARIETY OF SHAPES AND TEXTURES COMBINE TO MAKE A REAL STYLE STATEMENT.

When you need to take charge of a situation, this necklace will make you feel like an Amazon warrior queen. The violet and green color combo is inspired by my favorite flower, the wild violet...not to be confused with a shrinking violet... which you could never be and carry this piece off!

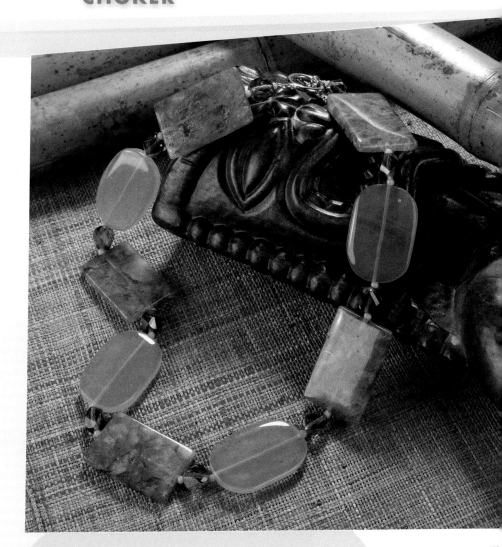

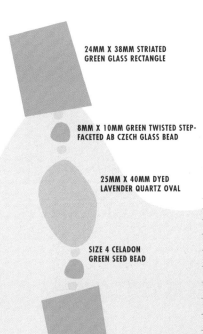

24MM X 38MM STRIATED
GREEN GLASS RECTANGLE

8MM X 10MM GREEN TWISTED STEP-
FACETED AB CZECH GLASS BEAD

25MM X 40MM DYED
LAVENDER QUARTZ OVAL

SIZE 4 CELADON
GREEN SEED BEAD

WHAT YOU WILL NEED

SUPPLIES
* **5** 24mm x 38mm striated green glass rectangles
* **5** 25mm x 40mm dyed lavender quartz ovals
* **10** 8mm x 10mm green twisted step-faceted AB Czech glass beads
* **1** tube size 4 celadon green seed beads
* large SP toggle clasp
* **2** no. 2 crimp tubes
* 22" (56cm) .018" (.46mm) 7 or 19 strand wire

TOOLS
* crimp tool
* flush cutters
* bead mat

RESOURCES: CZECH GLASS AND GLASS OVAL AND REC-TANGLE BEADS FROM GREAT CRAFT WORKS; TOGGLE, WIRE AND CRIMP TUBES FROM BEADALON; STERLING FINDINGS FROM MARVIN SCHWAB

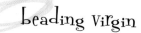 beading Virgin

26

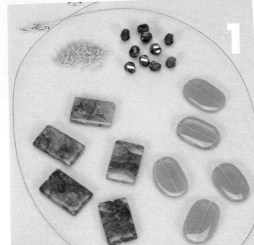

1

LAY OUT BEADS ON BEAD MAT

LAY OUT FIVE LARGE GREEN GLASS REC-
TANGLE BEADS AND FIVE OVAL LAVEN-
DER BEADS ON A BEAD MAT, ALONG
WITH ALL OF YOUR OTHER MATERIALS,
INCLUDING SEED BEADS, SMALL GREEN
CZECH GLASS BEADS, A 22" (56CM)
LENGTH OF WIRE, A CLASP AND TWO
CRIMP TUBES.

2

STRING BEADS AND ATTACH CLASP

ATTACH ONE END OF THE CLASP WITH A CRIMP TUBE (SEE TECH-
NIQUES, PAGE 14). STRING ON THE BEADS IN THE PATTERN AS
SHOWN IN THE DIAGRAM, BEGINNING WITH A SEED BEAD. WHEN
THE NECKLACE IS BEADED, THREAD THE WIRE THROUGH A CRIMP
TUBE AND THROUGH THE OTHER END OF THE CLASP. THREAD THE
WIRE BACK THROUGH THE CRIMP TUBE, HOLDING THE WIRE AND
PULLING ON IT TO MAKE THE BEADS FAIRLY TIGHT.

3

FINISH NECKLACE

BEFORE CRIMPING THE TUBE, FASTEN THE CLASP. ADJUST
THE WIRE LENGTH FOR PLAY SO THAT THE NECKLACE
MOVES BUT STILL RETAINS ITS SHAPE. CRIMP THE TUBE
AND TRIM AWAY THE EXCESS WIRE WITH FLUSH CUTTERS.

quickie: AMAZON EARRINGS

MAKE A STATEMENT WITH THESE BOLD MATCHING EAR-
RINGS. ANY COLOR-COORDINATED BEADS WILL WORK
HERE. YOU CAN ALSO LOOK FOR DECORATIVE EARRING
COMPONENTS TO ADD SOME SPICE TO YOUR DESIGNS.

LAY OUT EARRING COMPONENTS

LAY OUT ALL OF THE COMPONENTS FOR YOUR
EARRINGS ON YOUR WORK SURFACE OR ON A
BEAD MAT. THREAD A 8MM X 10MM STEP-
FACETED GREEN CZECH GLASS BEAD ONTO A
DECORATIVE SILVER LEAF BALINESE EYE PIN. CRE-
ATE A WRAPPED LOOP AT THE TOP. THREAD A
8MM AB OVAL LAVENDER FACETED CZECH
ROUND BEAD ONTO A HEAD PIN AND TURN
THE HEAD PIN AT THE TOP.

CREATE EARRING

ATTACH THE EARRING COMPO-
NENTS TOGETHER WITH PLIERS.
REPEAT TO MAKE THE SECOND
EARRING.

SPUNKY LIBRARIAN
POSY EYEGLASS HOLDER

CLIP YOUR READING GLASSES TO THIS FLOWERED EYEGLASS HOLDER AND YOU'LL INSTANTLY BE DAINTY, DEMURE AND DARLING, DAHLING.

If you're always hunting for your glasses, look adorable as you keep them at hand. Pair this accessory with a ladylike floral skirt, ballet flats and a classic twinset and make 'em think you're prim and proper.

7MM X 12MM PERIDOT TRANSLUCENT CZECH GLASS LEAF

7MM MULTICOLOR OPAL CZECH GLASS BUTTON FLOWER

JUMP RING

TOGGLE CIRCLE

4MM GREEN AB CZECH GLASS OVAL

LOBSTER CLASP

WHAT YOU WILL NEED

SUPPLIES
* **39** 7mm multicolor opal Czech glass button flowers
* **26** 7mm x 12mm peridot translucent Czech glass leaves
* **78** 4mm green AB Czech glass ovals
* gold-tone large toggle circle
* gold-tone lobster clasp
* **2** 8mm gold-tone jump rings
* **2** no. 2 gold-tone crimp tubes
* 29" (74cm) .018" (.46mm) 7 or 19 strand wire

TOOLS
* chain-nose pliers
* round-nose pliers
* crimp tool
* flush cutters
* bead board

RESOURCES: CZECH BEADS FROM YORK NOVELTY; FINDINGS AND WIRE FROM BEADALON

ATTACH CLASP AND THREAD ON FIRST BEADS

ATTACH A LOBSTER CLASP TO ONE END OF THE WIRE WITH A CRIMP TUBE (SEE TECHNIQUES, PAGE 14). THREAD THE FIRST SECTION OF BEADS ONTO THE WIRE IN THE PATTERN AS SHOWN ON PAGE 28, BEGINNING WITH A LEAF BEAD.

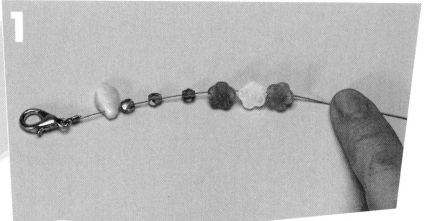

DESIGNER TIP

Let the beads guide you in new directions. These leaves and opal glass flowers with nesting abilities led me to imagine a vine holding my sunglasses. Gather up your beads; toss the rules out the window and play!

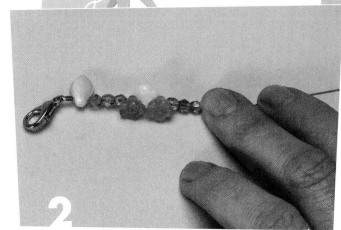

PUSH FLOWER BEADS TOGETHER

AFTER STRINGING ON THE FIRST SET OF FLOWER BEADS, STRING ON THE NEXT FEW BEADS AND THEN PUSH THEM AGAINST THE FLOWER BEADS SO THAT THE FLOWERS "NEST" INTO EACH OTHER. CONTINUE BEADING IN THE ESTABLISHED PATTERN UNTIL YOU REACH THE END.

ATTACH CIRCLE TOGGLE END

FINISH THE EYEGLASS HOLDER BY ATTACHING TWO 8MM GOLD-TONE JUMP RINGS TO THE END OF THE WIRE WITH A CRIMP TUBE. THEN ATTACH THE CIRCLE TOGGLE END TO THE FINAL JUMP RING. TO SECURE THE EYEGLASS HOLDER, ATTACH THE LOBSTER CLASP TO ONE OF THE JUMP RINGS. SLIDE ONE OF THE ARMS OF YOUR EYEGLASSES THROUGH THE LARGE TOGGLE CIRCLE AND YOU'LL ALWAYS KNOW WHERE THEY ARE.

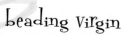
SEA DREAMER
WRAP NECKLACE

**INSPIRED BY OCEAN GLASS
I GATHERED FROM THE SOUTH-
ERN CALIFORNIA BEACHES,**
the soft shades of blue, lavender and
green in this necklace combine with
white-hot metal accents to create a
sassy modern design. Are you long-
ing for a tropical getaway? Toss this
on, close your eyes and imagine the
cabana boy bringing you a tasty cold
beverage in a pineapple!

**10MM X 14MM
LAVENDER DYED
QUARTZ OVAL**

**10MM X 14MM GREEN
DYED QUARTZ OVAL**

**10MM X 14MM
BLUE DYED
QUARTZ OVAL**

**THAI HILL
TRIBE LEAF
DANGLE**

**SIZE 11 BRIGHT
BLUE SEED BEAD**

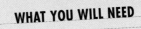

WHAT YOU WILL NEED

SUPPLIES
* ❋ **18** 10mm x 14mm blue dyed quartz ovals
* ❋ **19** 10mm x 14mm lavender dyed quartz ovals
* ❋ **19** 10mm x 14mm green dyed quartz ovals
* ❋ **1** tube size 11 bright blue frosted seed beads
* ❋ Thai Hill Tribe leaf dangle
* ❋ approx. 4" (10cm) medium stainless steel curb chain
* ❋ large SP toggle clasp
* ❋ **2** no. 2 sterling crimp tubes
* ❋ **3** sterling head pins
* ❋ 37" (94cm) .013" (.33mm) 19 or 49 strand wire

TOOLS
* ❋ chain-nose pliers
* ❋ round-nose pliers
* ❋ flush cutters

RESOURCES: BEADS AND HILL TRIBE SILVER FROM GREAT
CRAFT WORKS; CHAIN, WIRE AND CLASP FROM
BEADALON; SEED BEADS FROM BLUE MOON BEADS;
STERLING FINDINGS FROM MARVIN SCHWAB

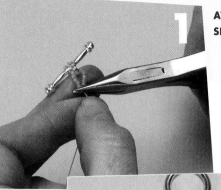

ATTACH CLASP WITH SEED BEAD LOOP

STRING A CRIMP TUBE ONTO ONE END OF THE 37" (94CM) WIRE. STRING ON 11 SEED BEADS. THREAD THE SEED BEADS THROUGH THE CLASP AND BACK THROUGH THE CRIMP TUBE TO CREATE A SMALL LOOP. USE CHAIN-NOSE PLIERS TO SMASH THE CRIMP TUBE SO THAT YOU DON'T BREAK THE SEED BEADS.

DESIGNER TIP

Adding seed beads on the wire around the clasp gives a polished look to your design. Wear this necklace a multitude of ways...doubling it up with the clasp and dangles hanging from the front, side or back of your neck. This gives you the look of a two-strand design without stringing two strands!

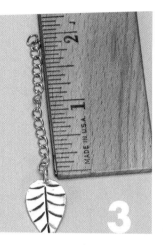

CREATE DANGLE COMPONENTS

THREAD THREE BEADS, ONE OF EACH COLOR, ONTO THREE HEAD PINS. CREATE A LOOP AT THE TOP OF EACH BEAD. ATTACH EACH BEADED DANGLE TO TWO LINKS OF STEEL CURB CHAIN. ALSO ATTACH A HILL TRIBE SILVER LEAF TO A 2" (5CM) LENGTH OF PREMADE STEEL CURB CHAIN.

STRING BEADS AND ATTACH OTHER END OF CLASP

STRING THE BEADS ONTO THE WIRE IN THE PATTERN AS SHOWN, THREADING ON A SEED BEAD IN BETWEEN THE LARGER BEADS. FINISH OFF THE NECKLACE BY REPEATING THE BEADED LOOP ON THE FINISHED END AND ATTACHING THE REMAINING END OF THE TOGGLE CLASP.

CREATE DANGLE

ATTACH THE BEADED DANGLES TO THE 2" (5CM) LENGTH OF STEEL CURB CHAIN WITH THE SILVER LEAF, ADDING ONE EVERY FOUR LINKS SO THAT THEY DANGLE FREELY FROM THE CHAIN. ATTACH THE LENGTH OF CHAIN WITH ITS DANGLES TO THE JUMP RING AT ONE END OF THE NECKLACE.

quickie: OCEAN GLASS BRACELET + EARRINGS

I used the same beads as in the necklace and looped them on head pins with premade steel chains to make a coordinating charm bracelet and some swingy earrings. (Look ahead to Charm School [page 54] if you need some tutoring.) How cute will you be?!

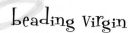
beading virgin

STARFIRE
LARIAT

THIS FIERY LARIAT PLAYS WITH WARM TONES AND COPPER FINDINGS TO CREATE A SPICY-HOT LOOK.

Lariats are incredibly versatile and easy to construct—you can even use this piece as a belt by adding more length. Wrap this around your neck when you plan to stir up some trouble...you feisty little vixen!

COPPER STAR

AB RED RECTANGLE

3MM INDIAN RED SWAROVSKI BICONE

3MM LIGHT PEACH SWAROVSKI BICONE

4MM HYACINTH SWAROVSKI BICONE

ORANGE FROSTED SQUARE GLASS BEAD

ORANGE FROSTED GLASS COIN BEAD

4MM ORANGE SWAROVSKI BICONE

COPPER GRAPE DANGLE

WHAT YOU WILL NEED

SUPPLIES

* **2** orange frosted glass square beads
* **2** orange frosted glass coin beads
* **52** copper stars
* **2** copper grape dangles
* **27** AB red rectangles
* **54** 3mm light peach Swarovski bicones
* **54** 4mm hyacinth Swarovski bicones
* **27** 3mm Indian red Swarovski bicones
* **2** 4mm orange Swarovski bicones
* **2** no. 2 gold crimp tubes
* **43"** (109cm) .015" (.38mm) 19 or 49 strand wire

TOOLS

* flush cutters
* crimp tool
* large bead board

RESOURCES: COPPER STARS FROM MARVIN SCHWAB; CRYSTALS FROM SWAROVSKI; COPPER FINDINGS, COIN AND SQUARE BEADS FROM BLUE MOON BEADS; AB RECTANGLES FROM JEWELRYSUPPLY.COM; WIRE AND CRIMPS FROM BEADALON

BEGIN NECKLACE

STRING A CRIMP TUBE ONTO A 43" (109CM) PIECE OF WIRE. NEXT STRING ON AN ORANGE BICONE CRYSTAL, TWO ORANGE FROSTED GLASS BEADS AND A DANGLE (AS SHOWN IN DIAGRAM) AND SLIDE THE WIRE BACK THROUGH THE BEADS.

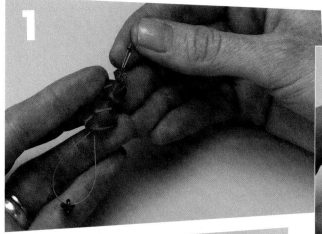

FINISH DANGLE

SLIDE THE WIRE BACK THROUGH THE CRIMP TUBE AND FLATTEN THE TUBE WITH A CRIMP TOOL. CUT OFF THE EXCESS WIRE TAIL WITH FLUSH CUTTERS.

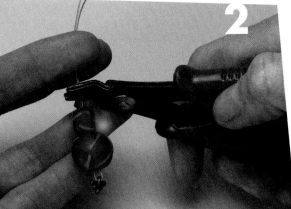

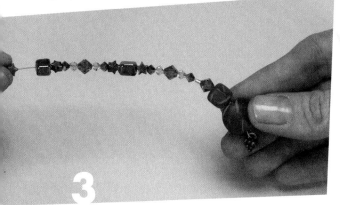

STRING BEADS

STRING THE BEADS ONTO THE LARIAT IN THE PATTERN AS SHOWN (THE REPEATING PATTERN BEGINS WITH THE 3MM INDIAN RED BICONE AND ENDS WITH THE SECOND COPPER STAR). WHEN YOU REACH THE END OF THE LARIAT, FINISH THE END IN THE SAME MANNER AS YOU BEGAN THE NECKLACE.

PATIENCE BOOSTER

When making a very long design like this one, it is smart to lay out the beads on a large bead board before you string. Laying the beads out in advance will ensure that you don't skip a bead in your pattern. Even with careful planning, you may occasionally miss a bead here or there. I let this kind of thing go...in the interest of sanity. If you just can't do that, then preparation is your friend.

quickie: STARFIRE EARRINGS

To make matching Starfire earrings, string crystals left over from the lariat onto copper head pins and make a wrapped loop at the top of each bead (see Techniques, pages 17–18). String one crystal onto an eye pin. Attach a jump ring to the top of each wrapped loop. Create one longer dangle by linking two smaller dangles together. Attach each dangle to one of the loops on a premade copper chandelier earring component.

ONE FISH,
KOI FISH NECKLACE

THIS CARVED AGATE KOI FISH BEGGED FOR AN ASIAN-INSPIRED COLOR PALETTE.
Although at first glance green and orange might not seem to go well together, the combination really works in this piece. After all, sometimes you have to take a few chances to make interesting designs. Free your inner art girl and be ready for the compliments you garner when you sport the complementary colors in this funky design.

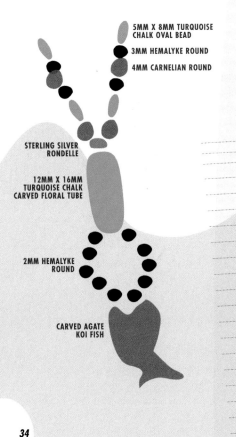

5MM X 8MM TURQUOISE CHALK OVAL BEAD

3MM HEMALYKE ROUND

4MM CARNELIAN ROUND

STERLING SILVER RONDELLE

12MM X 16MM TURQUOISE CHALK CARVED FLORAL TUBE

2MM HEMALYKE ROUND

CARVED AGATE KOI FISH

WHAT YOU WILL NEED

SUPPLIES
* carved agate koi fish
* **40** 3mm hemalyke rounds
* **10** 2mm hemalyke rounds
* **22** 4mm carnelian rounds
* **22** 5mm x 8mm turquoise chalk oval beads
* 12mm x 16mm turquoise chalk carved floral tube
* small sterling silver rondelle
* **2** no. 2 sterling silver crimp tubes
* sterling silver oval toggle clasp
* **2** 4mm silver jump rings
* 25" (63cm) .018" (.46mm) 7 or 19 strand wire

TOOLS
* chain-nose pliers
* round-nose pliers
* crimp tool
* flush cutters
* bead board

RESOURCES: GEMSTONE BEADS FROM FIRE MOUNTAIN GEMS AND BEADS; STERLING RONDELLES AND CRIMPS FROM MARVIN SCHWAB; STERLING TOGGLE FROM GREAT CRAFT WORKS; WIRE FROM BEADALON

BEGIN TO CREATE DANGLE

AFTER ATTACHING THE ROUND HALF OF THE TOGGLE CLASP WITH A CRIMP TUBE, THREAD ON THE FIRST HALF OF THE BEADS IN THE PATTERN AS SHOWN, STARTING WITH A TURQUOISE CHALK OVAL BEAD. WHEN YOU REACH THE HALFWAY MARK, THREAD ON A SILVER RONDELLE, THE CARVED CHALK TURQUOISE BEAD, FIVE 2MM HEMALYKE ROUNDS AND THE RED FISH, THREADING THE BEADED WIRE FROM FRONT TO BACK SO THE FISH WILL LAY FLAT.

DESIGNER TIP

Sometimes you have to step outside of your color comfort zone. Vibrant spring green and earthy orange look surprisingly wonderful together. The neutral and earthy tones in the carnelian and hemalyke help to balance out the brighter tone of the chalk turquoise.

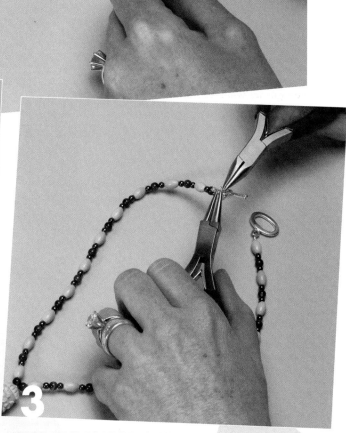

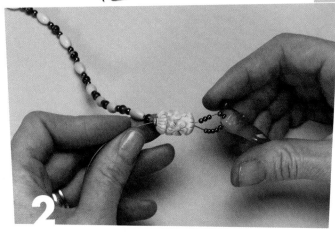

FINISH DANGLE

THREAD ON FIVE MORE 2MM HEMALYKE ROUNDS, THEN THREAD THE WIRE BACK UP THROUGH THE CHALK TURQUOISE BEAD AND THROUGH THE SILVER RONDELLE. AT THIS STAGE, MAKE SURE THAT THE WIRE IS SECURE, BUT NOT TOO TIGHT.

ATTACH CLASP TO NECKLACE END

BEAD THE SECOND HALF OF THE NECKLACE IN THE ESTABLISHED PATTERN. BEFORE ATTACHING THE BAR PIECE OF THE TOGGLE, ADD TWO JUMP RINGS TO ALLOW THE BAR TO FIT THROUGH THE RING. (WHEN BEADS ARE TOO LARGE, THE CIRCLE END OF THE TOGGLE CLASP CAN'T ALWAYS ACCOMMODATE THEM. ADDING EXTENSION CHAIN—IN THIS CASE, JUMP RINGS—SOLVES THIS DILEMMA.) USE A CRIMP TUBE TO ATTACH THE BEADED WIRE TO THE FINAL JUMP RING ON THE CLASP.

step it up, baby!

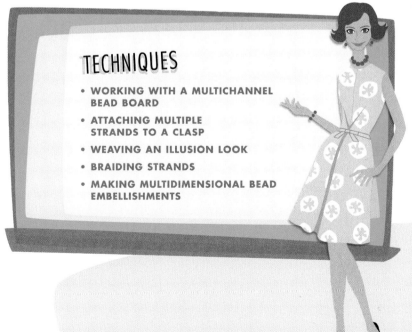

ARE YOU READY FOR SOME REAL FUN? NOW THAT YOU HAVE A HANDLE ON THE BASICS, WE'RE MOVING ON TO MULTISTRAND DESIGNS. TIGHTEN UP YOUR SEAT BELT, WE'RE PICKING UP SPEED!

You made it to chapter two, good for you! Here you will be introduced to multiple-strand designs and a veritable pu pu platter of approaches to working with more than one beaded strand. With these projects you are building on the technical and design skills you have gained and adding some new ones to your repertoire. Don't stress if some of the designs in this chapter seem a bit more complicated. Remember, everyone has to put her pants on one leg at a time, just like you. These pieces follow the same guideline. String one strand at a time and then link or weave them together. In the end, you'll have a piece of jewelry that looks far more complicated than it actually is.

"YOU WILL DO FOOLISH THINGS; DO THEM WITH ENTHUSIASM."
—COLETTE

TECHNIQUES

- **WORKING WITH A MULTICHANNEL BEAD BOARD**
- **ATTACHING MULTIPLE STRANDS TO A CLASP**
- **WEAVING AN ILLUSION LOOK**
- **BRAIDING STRANDS**
- **MAKING MULTIDIMENSIONAL BEAD EMBELLISHMENTS**

BROWNIE POINTS
NECKLACE

SEVERAL YEARS AGO, IN FRUSTRATION AT TRYING TO MAKE AN ILLUSION NECKLACE WITH CRIMP BEAD STATIONS,
I figured out how to weave two strands of wire through beads to get a similar effect with minimal effort. (Either I am a Zen master or incredibly lazy.) Since then, I have played around endlessly with this technique. In this piece, the colorful exposed wires become part of the design.

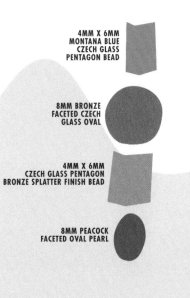

4MM X 6MM MONTANA BLUE CZECH GLASS PENTAGON BEAD

8MM BRONZE FACETED CZECH GLASS OVAL

4MM X 6MM CZECH GLASS PENTAGON BRONZE SPLATTER FINISH BEAD

8MM PEACOCK FACETED OVAL PEARL

WHAT YOU WILL NEED

SUPPLIES
* **11** 8mm peacock faceted oval pearls
* **11** 8mm bronze faceted Czech glass ovals
* **9** 4mm x 6mm Montana blue Czech glass pentagon beads
* **9** 4mm x 6mm Czech glass pentagon bronze splatter finish beads
* sterling silver toggle clasp
* **2** no. 2 sterling crimp tubes
* 22" (56cm) .018" (.46mm) 7 strand blue wire
* 22" (56cm) .018" (.46mm) 7 strand bronze wire

TOOLS
* chain-nose pliers
* crimp tool
* flush cutter
* bead board

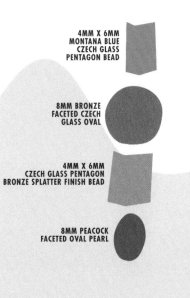

RESOURCES: FACETED PEARLS FROM THUNDERBIRD SUPPLY COMPANY; CZECH GLASS BEADS FROM YORK NOVELTY; STERLING FINDINGS FROM MARVIN SCHWAB; COLORED WIRE FROM BEADALON

ATTACH WIRES TO CLASP

CUT ONE 22" (56CM) LENGTH EACH OF BRONZE AND BLUE COLORED WIRE. THREAD BOTH STRANDS THROUGH ONE CRIMP TUBE AND THROUGH THE CLASP AND BACK THROUGH THE CRIMP TUBE, MAKING SURE THE WIRES DO NOT CROSS INSIDE THE CRIMP TUBE. CRIMP THE TUBE OVER BOTH OF THE WIRES AND SNIP OFF THE ENDS WITH FLUSH CUTTERS (SEE TECHNIQUES, PAGE 14).

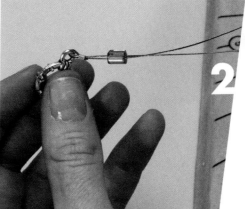

SLIDE ON BLUE GLASS TUBE

THREAD ONE MONTANA BLUE PENTAGON BEAD ONTO BOTH WIRES TO START, SLIDING IT DOWN TOWARD THE CLASP.

PATIENCE BOOSTER

Test the beads you intend to use to see what diameter of wire will double up inside of them while creating enough tension to station the beads along your design. If the holes are too small, the doubled wire won't fit. If the holes are too big, the beads will not remain in place.

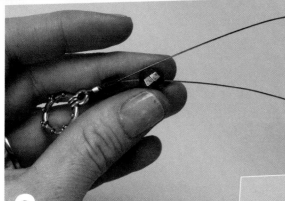

SLIDE ON BRONZE BEAD

THREAD A BRONZE FACETED OVAL BEAD ONTO THE BRONZE WIRE ONLY, SEPARATING THE TWO WIRES.

STRING ON BRONZE PENTAGON BEAD

THREAD ONE BRONZE PENTAGON SPLATTER FINISH BEAD ONTO BOTH WIRES, PUSHING THE BEAD DOWN TO CREATE A SLIGHT TENSION ON THE WIRE.

SLIDE ON PEARL BEAD

THREAD ONE FACETED PEACOCK PEARL
BEAD ONTO THE BLUE WIRE ONLY.

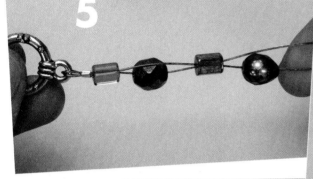

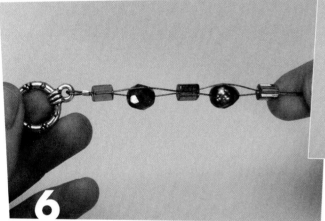

FINISH PATTERN WITH BLUE PENTAGON BEAD

THREAD ONE MONTANA BLUE GLASS PENTAGON BEAD ONTO
BOTH WIRES TO FINISH THE PATTERN. AS YOU BUILD, KEEP
ADJUSTING THE TENSION IN THE WIRES, BUT BE CAREFUL NOT
TO MAKE IT TOO TIGHT OR THE FINISHED PIECE WILL BE TOO
STIFF TO DRAPE PROPERLY.

FINISH NECKLACE

KEEP WORKING IN THE ESTABLISHED PATTERN UNTIL YOU REACH THE DESIRED
LENGTH. KEEP ADJUSTING THE BEADS ON THE WIRES AS YOU PROGRESS
THROUGH THE PATTERN, MAKING SURE THAT THEY ARE EQUIDISTANT. WHEN
YOU ARE FINISHED STRINGING, THREAD THE TWO WIRES THROUGH THE
CRIMP TUBE, THROUGH THE OTHER END OF THE CLASP AND BACK THROUGH
THE CRIMP TUBE. IF GETTING THE TWO WIRES BACK THROUGH THE CRIMP
TUBE IS A TIGHT FIT, YOU CAN USE YOUR CHAIN-NOSE PLIERS TO PULL THE
WIRES BACK THROUGH. USE THE CRIMP TOOL TO SECURE THE WIRES IN THE
CRIMP TUBE. CUT OFF THE ENDS WITH FLUSH CUTTERS.

quickie: BROWNIE POINTS EARRINGS

It's simple to create a dangle earring using beaded fancy Bali head pins and sterling eye pins. Use two 8mm
bronze faceted Czech glass ovals and two 4mm x 6mm Montana blue Czech glass pentagon beads left over
from the Brownie Points Necklace to make these matching earrings. The earthy colors and streamlined design
make them office-appropriate and denim-friendly.

1940s
NECKLACE + BRACELET SET

THERE IS ABSOLUTELY NO REASON THAT THESE COLORS SHOULD WORK TOGETHER... BUT SOMEHOW THEY DO.
I can't explain. I was playing with texture and color and came up with this design, which reminds me of something from the 1940s, when jewelry designers were really having fun. If you have some carved bakelite bangles, red platform shoes and a gabardine nipped-waist suit jacket, wear them with this necklace and bracelet set and some sexy jeans and a touch of red lipstick. You'll rock the house.

WHAT YOU WILL NEED

NECKLACE SUPPLIES
* **10** 8mm x10mm red Czech glass small windowpane beads
* **20** 8mm pink AB Czech glass rounds
* **9** 10mm x 14mm black Czech glass windowpane beads
* **9** 10mm lime Lucite or chartreuse cat's eye glass rounds
* small SP toggle clasp
* **20** no. 2 sterling crimp tubes
* **40"** (102cm) .015" (.38mm) 19 or 49 strand wire

BRACELET SUPPLIES
* **5** 8mm x 10mm red Czech glass small windowpane beads
* **10** 8mm pink AB Czech glass rounds
* **4** 10mm x 14mm black Czech glass windowpane beads
* **4** 10mm lime Lucite or chartreuse cat's eye glass rounds
* small toggle clasp
* **2** no. 2 sterling crimp tubes
* **20"** (51cm) .018" (.46mm) 7 strand red wire

TOOLS
* chain-nose pliers
* crimp tool
* flush cutters
* bead board

CRIMP TUBE

8MM PINK AB CZECH GLASS ROUND

8MM X 10MM RED CZECH GLASS WINDOWPANE BEAD

10MM X 14MM BLACK CZECH GLASS WINDOWPANE BEAD (BOTTOM)

10MM LIME LUCITE ROUND (TOP)

RESOURCES: CZECH GLASS FROM YORK NOVELTY; LUCITE FROM THE BEADIN' PATH; CAT'S EYE GLASS FROM BEADALON; FINDINGS AND WIRE FROM BEADALON

THE NECKLACE

THREAD ON FIRST SEGMENT OF BEADS

THREAD A CLASP ONTO THE 40" (102CM) WIRE STRAND. FOLD THE
WIRE IN HALF AND SLIDE THE CLASP DOWN SO THAT IT RESTS IN THE
FOLD. SLIDE A CRIMP TUBE ONTO BOTH WIRES, BRING IT DOWN CLOSE
TO THE CLASP AND SECURE THE CLASP WITH A CRIMP TUBE. STRING
THE FIRST THREE BEADS IN THE PATTERN (PINK, RED, PINK) ONTO BOTH
WIRES FOLLOWED BY A CRIMP TUBE. USE CHAIN-NOSE PLIERS (NOT
THE CRIMP TOOL) TO FLATTEN THE CRIMP TUBE SO IT IS PERPENDICULAR
TO THE GLASS BEADS, AS SHOWN BELOW.

THREAD ON STACKED BEADS

THREAD A FLAT BLACK BEAD ONTO THE BOTTOM WIRE
AND THE ROUND LIME BEAD ONTO THE TOP WIRE.

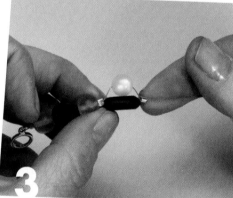

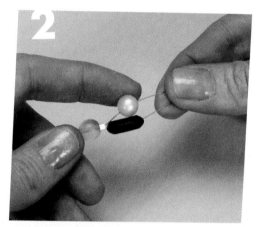

SMASH CRIMP TUBE

SMASH THE CRIMP TUBE VERTICALLY
WITH CHAIN-NOSE PLIERS, SO THAT IT
IS PERPENDICULAR TO THE CLASP.
BEFORE YOU CRIMP THE TUBE, MAKE
SURE YOU HAVE CORRECT TENSION.
THE WIRE WITH THE LIME BEAD WILL
BE LONGER, SO YOU NEED TO
ADJUST THE TENSION ACCORDINGLY.

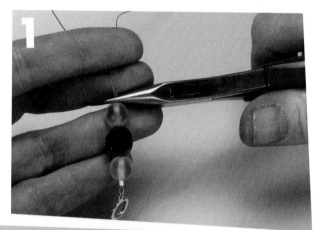

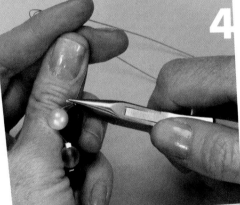

STACK BEADS

ADJUST THE BEADS SO THE LIME BEAD
RESTS ON TOP OF THE BLACK BEAD. SLIDE
A CRIMP TUBE ONTO BOTH WIRES AND
SLIDE IT FLUSH AGAINST THE STACKED
BEADS TO SECURE THEM.

FINISH NECKLACE

FINISH BEADING THE NECKLACE
IN THE ESTABLISHED PATTERN.
THREAD BOTH WIRES THROUGH
THE CRIMP TUBE, THROUGH THE
CLASP AND BACK THROUGH THE
CRIMP TUBE. SMASH THE CRIMP
TUBE WITH CHAIN-NOSE PLIERS
AND CUT OFF THE TAIL OF THE
WIRE WITH FLUSH CUTTERS.

AND THE **BRACELET**

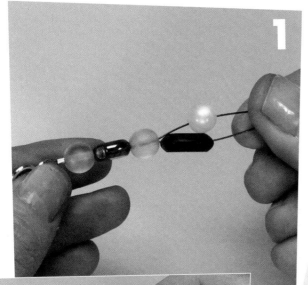

BEGIN STRINGING BRACELET

THREAD A CLASP ONTO A 20" (51CM) LENGTH OF WIRE
AND FOLD THE WIRE IN HALF SO THAT THE CLASP RESTS IN
THE FOLD. SLIDE A CRIMP TUBE ONTO THE FREE ENDS OF
THE WIRES AND SLIDE IT ALL THE WAY TO THE CLASP. CRIMP
THE CRIMP TUBE WITH THE CRIMP TOOL. STRING ON THE
FIRST GROUPING OF THREE BEADS. THREAD A BLACK BEAD
ON ONE WIRE AND A LIME BEAD ON THE OTHER WIRE,
ADJUSTING THEM SO THAT THE LIME BEAD RESTS ON TOP
OF THE BLACK BEAD.

DESIGNER TIP

The bracelet needs a larger diameter of wire and a slightly different
technique to achieve the same effect
as in the necklace. Modify your
materials to suit the task at hand.

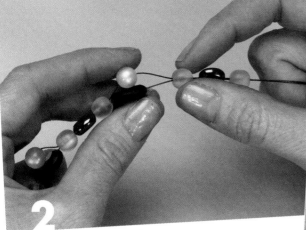

STRING BEADS IN PATTERN

CONTINUE STRINGING ON BEADS IN THE ESTABLISHED
PATTERN AND USE YOUR INDEX FINGER AND THUMB TO
HOLD THE BLACK AND LIME STACKED BEADS AS YOU
SLIDE THE NEXT GROUPING OF BEADS TOWARD THEM.

PUSH BEADS TOGETHER

PUSH THE PINK AND RED BEADS FLUSH AGAINST THE BLACK AND
LIME BEADS, ADJUSTING THE TENSION AS YOU SLIDE THE BEADS
ALONG. CONTINUE TO STRING THE REST OF THE BRACELET IN THE
ESTABLISHED PATTERN. BY THE END OF THE BRACELET, THE WIRE
WILL FORM INTO A CURVED SHAPE SINCE THE TOP WIRE IS A LITTLE
LONGER THAN THE BOTTOM WIRE. ATTACH THE OTHER END OF
THE CLASP WITH A CRIMP TUBE TO FINISH THE BRACELET.

BAHAMA MAMA
BRAIDED NECKLACE

IMAGINE CAPTURING THE BEAUTY OF THE OCEAN AND STRINGING IT ON A WIRE.
This beautiful celebration of color and texture will bring your wardrobe to life with the vividness of the ocean. Braiding the strands gives a dimensional and organic feel to the finished design. Wear this with a sexy swimsuit, Jackie O. sunglasses, spiky heels and a large-brimmed straw hat to your next pool party and release your inner diva!

12MM X 16MM RECONSTITUTED TURQUOISE ROUNDED RECTANGLE

10MM X 14MM CHALK TURQUOISE OVAL

10MM BLUE QUARTZ CHICLET BEAD

5MM BLUE STRIATED CZECH GLASS RONDELLE

WHAT YOU WILL NEED

SUPPLIES
* **241** 5mm blue striated Czech glass rondelles
* **15** 12mm x 16mm reconstituted turquoise rounded rectangles
* **10** 10mm x 14mm chalk turquoise ovals
* **23** 10mm blue quartz chiclet beads
* SP textured toggle clasp
* **6** no. 2 sterling crimp tubes
* **2** 4mm jump rings
* **3** 30" (76cm) lengths of .018" (.46mm) 7 or 19 strand wire

TOOLS
* chain-nose pliers
* round-nose pliers
* crimp tool
* flush cutters
* multichannel bead board

RESOURCES: CZECH GLASS FROM YORK NOVELTY; TURQUOISE FROM PHOENIX JEWELRY & PARTS; BLUE QUARTZ FROM THUNDERBIRD SUPPLY; STERLING FINDINGS FROM MARVIN SCHWAB; WIRE FROM BEADALON; EARRING COMPONENTS FROM FIRE MOUNTAIN GEMS

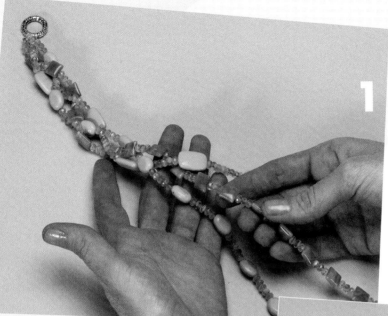

1 BEAD AND BRAID STRANDS

ATTACH THREE STRANDS OF WIRE TO ONE END OF A TOGGLE CLASP USING A CRIMP TUBE FOR EACH STRAND. BEAD EACH STRAND IN THE PATTERN AS SHOWN ON PAGE 44 AND SECURE THE ENDS OF EACH WIRE STRAND WITH A CRIMP TUBE. BRAID THE THREE BEADED STRANDS TOGETHER LOOSELY—IF YOU BRAID THEM TOO TIGHTLY, THE NECKLACE WILL BE TOO STIFF TO WEAR.

PATIENCE BOOSTER

The tricky part of this design is crimping off each of the beaded strands. Don't rush this or you will be restringing for sure, snark. Take your time and save yourself the stress!

2 ATTACH CLASP AND ADJUST BRAID

ATTACH THE FREE ENDS OF THE THREE BRAIDED STRANDS TO A JUMP RING USING ROUND-NOSE AND CHAIN-NOSE PLIERS. CLOSE THE JUMP RING TO SECURE IT. OPEN A SECOND JUMP RING AND ATTACH IT TO THE FIRST JUMP RING. ATTACH THE SECOND JUMP RING TO THE BAR END OF THE TOGGLE CLASP. STRETCH THE NECKLACE OUT ON YOUR WORK SURFACE AND USE YOUR FINGERS TO MAKE SURE THE BRAID IS EVENLY SPACED.

quickie: BAHAMA MAMA EARRINGS

Here is a really quick and fun earring using a three-loop gypsy earring hoop. Attach one each of the larger beads on looped head pins to each earring loop using your pliers to open and close the loops to the side. (As with a jump ring, you don't want to break the loop by opening it improperly.) Oh waiter, won't you refill my pineapple, please?

MORGAN LE FEY
ENCHANTED NECKLACE

LET ME BEGIN BY SAYING THAT I LOVE DRAGONFLIES.
Let me also say that I was a strange kid...surprised? I figured out when I was five that if you hit a dragonfly with a beach ball, it would die and be perfectly preserved. I saved up a whole bunch of them and put them in my Dad's sock drawer while on a beach vacation. Dad was none too happy. Now that I don't collect dead bugs anymore, I am thrilled whenever I find a cool new dragonfly bead. In this design, Thai Hill Tribe silver dragonflies float on strands of pearls and chain to create a lovely romantic design.

METAL STAMPED DIAMOND BEAD

3MM HEMALYKE ROUND

4MM MAUVE POTATO PEARL

4MM CREAM GREEN TEA POTATO PEARL

METAL CROISSANT-SHAPED BEAD

SMALL THAI HILL TRIBE DRAGONFLY

WHAT YOU WILL NEED

SUPPLIES
* **92** 3mm brown rice pearls
* **30** 4mm cream green tea colored potato pearls
* **16** 4mm mauve colored potato pearls
* **6** metal stamped diamond beads
* **6** metal croissant-shaped beads
* **30** 3mm hemalyke rounds
* **2** small Thai Hill Tribe dragonflies
* large Thai Hill Tribe dragonfly
* **72** links of elongated stainless steel chain
* large SP toggle clasp
* **4** no. 2 crimp tubes
* **2** 22" (56cm) lengths .015" (.38mm) 7, 19 or 49 strand wire
* clear tape

TOOLS
* chain-nose pliers
* round-nose pliers
* flush cutters
* crimp tool
* multichannel bead board

RESOURCES: PEARLS FROM THUNDERBIRD SUPPLY; HEMALYKE ROUNDS FROM FIRE MOUNTAIN GEMS; METAL BEADS FROM BLUE MOON BEADS; HILL TRIBE DRAGONFLIES FROM GREAT CRAFT WORKS; WIRE, CHAIN AND CLASP FROM BEADALON

STRING ON BEADS AND FIRST DRAGONFLY

ATTACH ONE END OF EACH 22" (56CM) LENGTH OF WIRE TO ONE END OF THE CLASP USING A CRIMP TUBE FOR EACH STRAND. STRING THE BROWN RICE PEARLS ONTO ONE STRAND AND TAPE THE END TO SECURE THE BEADS. STRING THE COLORED PEARLS AND SILVER BEADS ONTO THE SECOND STRAND IN THE PATTERN AS SHOWN. BECAUSE OF LIMITED SPACE, THE DIAGRAM DOES NOT START FROM THE BEGINNING. WHEN YOU STRING, COMPLETE TWO FULL CYCLES OF THE SEQUENCE BEFORE SLIDING ON ONE OF THE SMALLER DRAGONFLIES (ONLY ONE CYCLE IS SHOWN IN THE DIAGRAM). AFTER THE DRAGONFLY, PICK UP THE PATTERN FROM THE BEGINNING (THE DRAGONFLY WILL BE SANDWICHED BETWEEN TWO GREEN PEARLS).

PATIENCE BOOSTER

Always check your wires before crimping to keep them from crossing inside of the crimp tube. Also make sure you line the tube up properly within the crimp tool. There is nothing more depressing than finishing a complicated design, crimping your wire and watching your beads fly across the room.

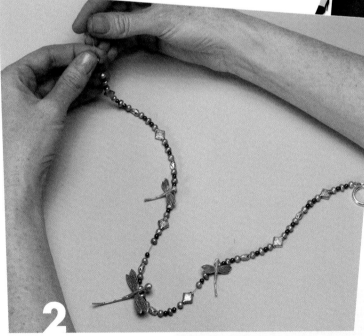

FINISH STRINGING

CONTINUE STRINGING THE REMAINDER OF THE BEADS IN THE ESTABLISHED PATTERN. WHEN YOU REACH THE CENTER OF THE NECKLACE, STRING ON THE LARGE DRAGONFLY, AND CONTINUE THE PATTERN, STRINGING ON ANOTHER SMALLER DRAGONFLY SYMMETRICALLY. REPEAT THE PATTERN AS SHOWN IN THE DIAGRAM UNTIL THE TWO HALVES OF THE NECKLACE ARE EVEN. TAPE OFF THE END.

ATTACH CHAIN

USE CRIMP TUBES TO ATTACH THE TWO BEADED STRANDS TO THE OTHER END OF THE CLASP. MEASURE OUT A LENGTH OF THE CHAIN TO THE SAME LENGTH AS THE OTHER TWO BEADED STRANDS AND USE PLIERS TO OPEN AND CLOSE THE CHAIN END LINKS USING THE JUMP RING METHOD. ATTACH ONE END OF THE CHAIN TO ONE END OF THE CLASP. ATTACH THE OTHER END OF THE CHAIN TO THE OTHER END OF THE CLASP. (THE CHAIN SHOULD BE ATTACHED ON TOP.)

GREY SCALE
NECKLACE

FASHION GODDESS COCO CHANEL INSPIRED DAYTIME GLAMOUR BY PILING ON MULTIPLE STRANDS OF PEARLS IN THE 1930s.
In this necklace I have updated her look with fabulous Swarovski crystal light grey pearls and Swarovski crystal crosses. Feel free to change up the color palette and to add more pearl strands if you so desire. High style meets hip in this necklace fit for a true Fashionista.

SIZE 15 TOHO SEED BEAD

4MM LIGHT GREY SWAROVSKI CRYSTAL PEARL

20MM SWAROVSKI CRYSTAL CROSS

WHAT YOU WILL NEED

SUPPLIES
* **74** 4mm light grey Swarovski crystal pearls
* **3** 20mm Swarovski crystal crosses
* **228** size 15 Toho grey seed beads
* extra large sterling lobster clasp
* 6mm oval sterling jump ring
* **3** 6mm SP jump rings
* 8mm SP jump ring
* **8** no. 2 crimp tubes
* **2** 19" (48cm) lengths and 2 20" (51cm) lengths .013" (.33mm) 49 strand wire

TOOLS
* chain-nose pliers
* round-nose pliers
* crimp tool
* flush cutters
* multistrand bead board

RESOURCES: CRYSTAL FROM SWAROVSKI; WIRE, JUMP RINGS AND TOHO SEED BEADS FROM BEADALON; STERLING FINDINGS FROM MARVIN SCHWAB

BEAD FOUR STRANDS, ADD FIRST CROSS

ATTACH ALL FOUR STRANDS OF WIRE TO A 6MM JUMP RING, USING A CRIMP TUBE TO SECURE EACH WIRE (SEE TECHNIQUES, PAGE 15). ATTACH THE JUMP RING TO THE LOBSTER CLASP. BEAD EACH OF THE WIRES WITH SWAROVSKI GLASS CRYSTAL PEARLS AND GREY SEED BEADS, BEGINNING WITH A CRYSTAL PEARL AND ALTERNATING BETWEEN THE TWO. BEAD THE TWO SHORTER STRANDS TO 15" (38CM), AND THE TWO LONGER STRANDS TO 16" (41CM). ATTACH EACH END OF EACH STRAND WITH A CRIMP TUBE TO A 6MM OVAL JUMP RING. OPEN A 6MM JUMP RING AND USE IT TO ATTACH A CROSS PENDANT RIGHT OVER THE 35TH BEAD FROM ONE END ON ONE OF THE 16" (41CM) STRANDS.

PATIENCE BOOSTER

Hey, slow down there little missy! Don't be in a hurry, or you will skip beads! With a highly repetitive pattern, it is easy to drop a seed bead or two. Take your time and check over your work before crimping to avoid silly mistakes.

CLOSE SMALL JUMP RING

CLOSE THE JUMP RING WITH ROUND-NOSE AND CHAIN-NOSE PLIERS. THE CROSS SHOULD BE SECURELY ATTACHED SO THAT IT DOES NOT MOVE AROUND ON THE CHAIN. REPEAT WITH ANOTHER CROSS ON THE SAME STRAND, OVER THE 35TH BEAD FROM THE OTHER END.

ATTACH FINAL CROSS

ATTACH THE FINAL CROSS ONTO THE CENTER OF THE SECOND 16" (41CM) STRAND USING AN 8MM JUMP RING. THIS CROSS SHOULD SLIDE BACK AND FORTH OVER THE BEADS.

PSYCHEDELIC
NECKLACE

PSYCHEDELIC ORANGE, YELLOW AND AQUA COMBINE IN THIS RETRO-CHIC GRADUATED THREE-STRAND NECKLACE.
A handmade glass daisy pendant takes center stage. Don some pale pink lips, way-too-big false eyelashes, go-go boots and a Pucci-esque mini to create a pop art vibe. Now go find a platform on the dance floor and channel your inner Edie Sedgewick.

6MM BLUE CRACKLE CZECH
GLASS FUNKY SHAPE BEAD

6MM YELLOW INSIDE
COLOR CZECH GLASS
FUNKY SHAPE BEAD

10MM CORAL
OPAQUE CZECH
GLASS FUNKY
SHAPE BEAD

WHAT YOU WILL NEED

SUPPLIES
* **40** 10mm coral opaque Czech glass funky shape beads
* **40** 6mm yellow inside color Czech glass funky shape beads
* **76** 6mm blue crackle Czech glass funky shape beads
* blown glass yellow flower Czech glass teardrop (approx. 30mm x 15mm)
* **2** 3-to-1 filigree connectors
* small SP toggle clasp
* **4** 4mm SP jump rings
* 6mm SP jump ring
* **6** no. 2 sterling crimp tubes
* **3** 22" (56cm) lengths .018" (.46mm) 7, 19 or 49 strand wire

TOOLS
* chain-nose pliers
* round-nose pliers
* crimp tool
* flush cutter
* multichannel bead board

RESOURCES: PENDANT AND BEADS FROM CRAFT WORKS; FINDINGS AND WIRE FROM BEADALON

LAY OUT BEADS ON BEAD BOARD

LAY OUT ALL OF THE BEADS ON THE BEAD BOARD IN THE PATTERN AS SHOWN. (NOTE THAT THE MIDDLE STRAND BEGINS WITH A CORAL BEAD.) IN THE CENTER OF THE LONGEST STRAND, LEAVE OUT THE YELLOW BEAD BETWEEN THE TWO BLUE BEADS (THE YELLOW PENDANT WILL GO THERE). ALL THREE STRANDS WILL REACH APPROXIMATELY TO THE OUTSIDE 8½" (22CM) MARK. EACH STRAND IS A SLIGHTLY DIFFERENT LENGTH TO CREATE A NESTED OR GRADUATED EFFECT.

STRING STRANDS AND ATTACH TO CONNECTOR

ATTACH A 22" (56CM) STRAND OF WIRE TO THE OUTSIDE HOLE IN THE 3-TO-1 FILIGREE CONNECTOR WITH A CRIMP TUBE. THREAD BEADS ONTO THE STRAND IN THE PATTERN AS SHOWN. ATTACH THE END TO AN OUTSIDE HOLE IN THE SECOND CONNECTOR. REPEAT FOR THE REMAINING TWO STRANDS. (MAKE SURE THE STRANDS ARE GRADUATED WHEN YOU ATTACH THEM—THE LONGEST STRAND SHOULD BE ON THE OUTSIDE.) ADD THE CLASP TO THE CONNECTOR USING ONE JUMP RING TO CONNECT THE CIRCLE END OF THE CLASP AND A CHAIN OF THREE JUMP RINGS TO ATTACH THE CONNECTOR TO THE BAR END OF THE CLASP.

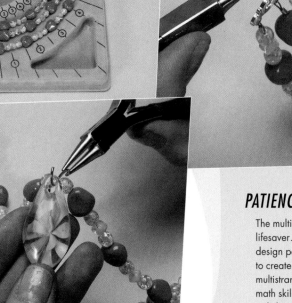

ADD PENDANT

SLIDE THE YELLOW PENDANT ONTO A 6MM JUMP RING AND ATTACH THE JUMP RING TO THE CENTER OF THE BOTTOM STRAND USING ROUND-NOSE AND CHAIN-NOSE PLIERS.

PATIENCE BOOSTER

The multichannel bead board is a lifesaver...you can map out your design pattern and strand length to create a perfectly proportioned multistrand design without any math skills whatsoever. For the right-brained among you...say oh yeah! If you would rather do the math, go for it!

beading Vixen

MOVIE MAVEN
BRACELET

EVERY ONCE IN A WHILE, I RUN ACROSS A BEAD THAT IS PERFECT WITHOUT ANY OTHER EMBELLISHMENTS.
I loved these oddly shaped frosted kidney beads on the hank. So I just strung up a bunch of them to make a chunky cool bracelet. The glossy side of the beads catches the light and creates an interesting dimension. Feel free to create a similar look with any beads that strike your fancy, Fancy.

WHAT YOU WILL NEED

SUPPLIES

❋ approx. **180** 7mm x 5mm purple frosted AB Czech glass kidney beads
❋ three-strand filigree box clasp
❋ **12** no. 2 sterling crimp tubes
❋ **6** 12" (30cm) lengths .018" (.46mm) 19 or 49 strand wire
❋ clear tape

TOOLS

❋ crimp tool
❋ flush cutters
❋ bead mat

RESOURCES: BEADS FROM YORK NOVELTY; WIRE, FINDINGS AND FLUSH CUTTERS FROM BEADALON

PATIENCE BOOSTER

The more bead strands you use for a bracelet, the longer the individual strands will need to be to accommodate your wrist. It's math again…sigh. Keep testing the design on your wrist as you work and before you commit with the crimp tubes to save yourself from restringing later.

ATTACH WIRE STRANDS TO THREE-STRAND SNAP CLASP

ATTACH SIX 12" (30CM) LENGTHS OF WIRE TO THE THREE-STRAND CLASP, SECURING TWO STRANDS OF WIRE TO EACH LOOP IN THE CLASP. EACH WIRE SHOULD BE SECURED BY ONE CRIMP TUBE. USE FLUSH CUTTERS TO SNIP OFF EXCESS WIRE. PLACE YOUR BEADS ON A BEAD MAT TO KEEP THEM FROM RUNNING AWAY.

STRING BRACELET

STRING 30 PURPLE BEADS ONTO EACH STRAND. THE BEADS ARE ODDLY SHAPED, SO JUST STRING THEM ON, AND THEY WILL FALL NICELY. AS YOU FINISH STRINGING EACH STRAND, TAPE OFF THE END SO YOU DON'T LOSE ANY BEADS.

FINISH BRACELET

ATTACH THE REMAINING BEADED STRANDS TO THE CLASP. UPON UNCLASPING THE BRACELET YOU SHOULD SEE SOME EXTRA WIRE VISIBLE AT THE ENDS OF THE STRANDS. FRET NOT, THIS IS CALLED "PLAY." IF THERE ISN'T ENOUGH PLAY, THE BRACELET WILL NOT BE FLEXIBLE ENOUGH TO BEND AND DRAPE PROPERLY.

ATTACH WIRES TO OTHER END OF CLASP

BEFORE ATTACHING THE WIRES TO THE CLASP, CLOSE THE CLASP. ATTACH THE FIRST STRAND TO THE OTHER END OF THE CLASP WITH A CRIMP TUBE AND THE CRIMP TOOL. BEFORE YOU BEGIN TO CRIMP, TAKE YOUR TIME TO PULL THE WIRE THROUGH THE CRIMP TUBE TO MAKE SURE THE TENSION IS CORRECT.

charm school

WHO NEEDS PRINCE CHARMING WHEN YOU CAN CHARM YOURSELF WITH THESE DELICIOUS DESIGNS? LEARN HOW TO EMBELLISH PINS, EARRINGS, BRACELETS AND CHOKERS WITH BEAUTI-FUL BEADED DANGLES AND PUT A LITTLE SASS IN YOUR WARDROBE. SINCE YOU ARE BECOMING A BEAD MASTER, YOU MAY WANT TO PLOP DOWN THE COLD CASH FOR SOME FANCIER TOOLS.

Now for something completely different, this chapter is about integrating movement into your designs. Presented for your beading enjoyment is a cornucopia of lovely beaded charms, dangles and chains for pins, earrings, necklaces and bracelets. Adding charms to jewelry pieces is a great way to create the feel you're after—from delicate pearl dangles made with wrapped wire to retro-esque silver beach images. Once you graduate from charm school (unless you become a charm school dropout, that is) you will be well on your way to becoming a serious jewelry arti-san. Aren't you proud?

"ODD HOW THE CREATIVE POWER AT ONCE BRINGS THE WHOLE UNIVERSE TO ORDER."
—VIRGINIA WOOLF

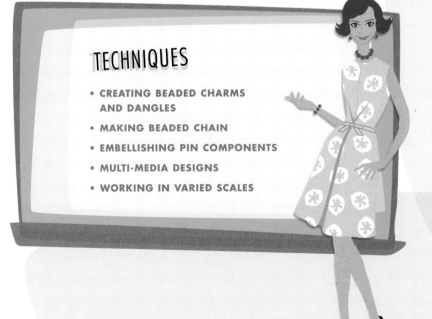

TECHNIQUES

- **CREATING BEADED CHARMS AND DANGLES**
- **MAKING BEADED CHAIN**
- **EMBELLISHING PIN COMPONENTS**
- **MULTI-MEDIA DESIGNS**
- **WORKING IN VARIED SCALES**

ISLAND GIRL
KILT PIN

CAN YOU SENSE A THEME IN THIS BOOK...I LOVE THE BEACH. ONE DAY I PLAN TO GO THERE AND NEVER RETURN.

For now, I just wear a lot of tropical-inspired baubles and ensembles (pronounced as my daughter does each morning...en-som-blays!). This pin is a perfect way to bring a little beach into your winter wardrobe. Pearls, mother of pearl, metal and crystal are united in a symphony of iridescent shine.

8MM X 14MM MOP DIAMOND BEAD

BLACK DIAMOND SWAROVSKI TEARDROP

4MM INDICOLITE SWAROVSKI BICONE

3MM WHITE FRESHWATER PEARL

9MM X 6MM BLACK DIAMOND SWAROVSKI SQUARE CHANNEL CHAIN

MOP CARVED MEDIUM FLOWER

WHAT YOU WILL NEED

SUPPLIES
* **1** black lip oyster mother of pearl (MOP) carved medium flower
* **2** 8mm x 14mm black lip oyster mother of pearl (MOP) diamond beads
* **6** links 9mm x 6mm black diamond Swarovski square channel chain
* **1** black diamond Swarovski teardrop
* **2** 3mm white freshwater pearls
* **2** 4mm indicolite Swarovski bicones
* 6mm indicolite Swarovski bicone
* metal SP kilt pin
* **8** 24-gauge sterling head pins
* **2** 4mm jump rings
* 6mm jump ring

TOOLS
* round-nose pliers
* chain-nose pliers
* flush cutters
* bead reamer

RESOURCES: MOP FLOWER, MOP DIAMONDS, PEARLS AND BEADS FROM FIRE MOUNTAIN GEMS; KILT PIN, HEAD PINS AND JUMP RINGS FROM JEWELRYSUPPLY.COM; SWAROVSKI BEADS AND CHANNEL CHAIN FROM SWAROVSKI

PATIENCE BOOSTER

When creating double-looped dangle components, make sure to bend each loop to the opposite direction. One loop should go toward the left, and one to the right. That way, all of the components, when linked, will lay correctly.

REAM BEAD

RUN THE ELECTRIC BEAD REAMER BACK AND FORTH INSIDE OF THE MOTHER OF PEARL DIAMOND BEADS TO MAKE SURE THE OPENING IS BIG ENOUGH TO ACCOMMODATE THE HEAD PIN WIRE.

BUILD DANGLES

CREATE DANGLES BY THREADING EACH BEAD ON AN EYE PIN OR A HEAD PIN. ONE MOP DIAMOND AND THE SWAROVSKI TEARDROP NEED BOTH TOP AND BOTTOM LOOPS. ALL OF THE OTHER BEADS WILL BE THREADED ONTO HEAD PINS AND WILL HAVE ONE LOOP AT THE TOP.

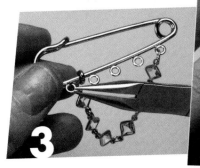

ATTACH CHAIN TO PIN

ATTACH SIX LINKS OF SPARKLY CHAIN (WITH PREATTACHED JUMP RINGS) TO THE FIRST AND LAST LOOPS ON THE KILT PIN USING ROUND-NOSE AND CHAIN-NOSE PLIERS.

ATTACH LONG DANGLE

LINK A MOTHER OF PEARL DIAMOND AND A BLACK DIAMOND TEARDROP ON DOUBLE-LOOPED HEAD PINS. ATTACH THE DANGLE TO THE FIRST LOOP ON THE PIN. ATTACH A JUMP RING TO THE BOTTOM OF THE DANGLE AND LINK ONE PEARL AND TWO BICONE CRYSTALS TO IT.

ADD FLOWER

AFTER ATTACHING THE DANGLES AS SHOWN IN THE DIAGRAM, ADD ON THE MOTHER OF PEARL CARVED FLOWER. THREAD A 6MM JUMP RING THROUGH THE DRILL HOLE AND CONNECT IT TO TWO LINKED 4MM JUMP RINGS. ATTACH THE TOP JUMP RING TO THE CENTER LINK OF THE CRYSTAL CHANNEL CHAIN.

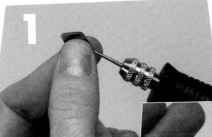

quickie: ROCKABILLY FILLY KILT PIN

Kilt pins offer designers an array of options. Here I used huge vintage German glass teardrops and Swarovski chaton head pins on varied lengths of chain for a fun and funky look.

SOFT ROCK DIVA
NECKLACE

CHARMS AND CHAINS ARE EVERYWHERE THESE DAYS.
In this piece, pastel colors soften the edgy look of the metal and make a necklace that will become a wardrobe staple. Replace the beads with hardware store odds and ends for an industrial vibe or use the head pin technique introduced here to attach funky vintage buttons. The key is to find your own creative voice as you master your technique.

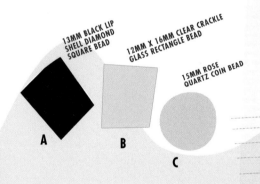

A — 13MM BLACK LIP SHELL DIAMOND SQUARE BEAD

B — 12MM X 16MM CLEAR CRACKLE GLASS RECTANGLE BEAD

C — 15MM ROSE QUARTZ COIN BEAD

WHAT YOU WILL NEED

SUPPLIES
* **5** 15mm front to back drilled rose quartz coin beads
* **6** 12mm x 16mm clear crackle glass rectangle beads
* **6** 13mm black lip shell diamond square beads
* **59** links elongated steel cable chain
* embellished SP square toggle clasp
* **17** 22-gauge sterling head pins

TOOLS
* chain-nose pliers
* round-nose pliers
* flush cutters

RESOURCES: ROSE QUARTZ BEADS FROM PHOENIX JEWELRY AND PARTS; BLACK SHELL BEADS FROM GREAT CRAFT WORKS; TOGGLE CLASP FROM BLUE MOON BEADS; STEEL CHAIN FROM BEADALON
PINKY SWEAR COMPONENTS: FIRE MOUNTAIN GEMS, CRYSTALS FROM SWAROVSKI

BEGIN TO CREATE DANGLES

ON BEADS DRILLED FRONT TO BACK, INSERT THE HEAD PIN AND USE YOUR FINGERS TO BEND THE WIRE UP 90° SO THAT IT WILL DANGLE CORRECTLY.

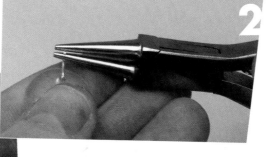

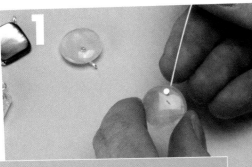

FINISH DANGLES

CUT THE HEAD PIN SO THAT THERE IS ABOUT ¼" (1CM) OF WIRE LEFT ABOVE THE BEAD. HOLD THE BEAD BETWEEN YOUR THUMB AND FOREFINGER AND USE YOUR ROUND-NOSE PLIERS TO CREATE A LOOP IN THE HEAD PIN WIRE BY TWIST-ING THE PLIERS TOWARD YOUR-SELF TO MAKE THE LOOP.

PATIENCE BOOSTER

Save your head pin rem-nants—you'll need them later. It might seem like a pain, but saving the scraps will save you money.

LINK DANGLES TO CHAIN

ADD THE BEADS EVERY FOUR LINKS IN THE PATTERN A, B, C AS SHOWN IN THE DIAGRAM. TO ATTACH EACH BEAD DANGLE, USE ROUND-NOSE AND CHAIN-NOSE PLIERS.

ADD CLASP

USE THE CHAIN-NOSE AND ROUND-NOSE PLIERS TO ADD THE CLASP. REMEMBER, IF USING A TOGGLE CLASP, THE BAR END MUST BE ATTACHED WITH JUMP RINGS SO THAT IT HAS ENOUGH LEEWAY TO FIT THROUGH THE CIRCLE END.

quickie: PINKY SWEAR

A ready-made hot pink multistrand cable choker looks fab with sterling findings and two-toned pink Swarovski crystal drops. A sterling connector component gets flipped upside down and attached to another with jump rings to create an adorable pendant. Break the rules for innovative design ideas!

DAINTY DEBUTANTE
CHARM BRACELET

WITH ITS SPARKLE AND PLAY, THIS BRACELET IS FIT FOR THE COUNTRY CLUB SET.

Muffy Elizabeth Vandersmith III has nothing on you, girl. With a lavender polo shirt, driving mocs, khaki skirt and a cashmere sweater tossed casually over your shoulders, no one will ever guess that you weren't born with a silver spoon in your mouth.

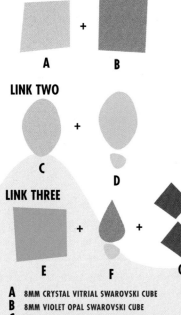

LINK ONE

A + B

LINK TWO

C + D

LINK THREE

E + F + G

A 8MM CRYSTAL VITRIAL SWAROVSKI CUBE
B 8MM VIOLET OPAL SWAROVSKI CUBE
C 8MM X 12MM CZECH GLASS SPLATTER FINISH PURPLE WINDOWPANE BEAD
D 8MM X 12MM CZECH GLASS SPLATTER FINISH GREEN WINDOWPANE BEAD, BALINESE SILVER FANCY HEAD PIN
E 8MM KHAKI SWAROVSKI CUBE
F 9MM X 6MM VIOLET SWAROVSKI TEARDROP, KHAKI SWAROVSKI CHATON HEAD PIN
G 6MM RUST METALLIC CZECH GLASS SMOOTH BICONE BEAD, 6MM BROWN METALLIC CZECH GLASS SMOOTH BICONE BEAD

RESOURCES: SWAROVSKI CRYSTAL HEAD PINS AND BEADS FROM JEWELRYSUPPLY.COM; CZECH GLASS FROM YORK NOVELTY; STERLING FINDINGS FROM MARVIN SCHWAB; TWISTED TOGGLE CLASP FROM GREAT CRAFT WORKS; FIGARO CHAIN FROM FIRE MOUNTAIN GEMS

WHAT YOU WILL NEED

SUPPLIES

* **4** 8mm crystal vitrial medium Swarovski cubes
* **4** 8mm violet opal Swarovski cubes
* **3** 8mm khaki Swarovski cubes
* **3** 6mm brown metallic Czech glass smooth bicone beads
* **3** 6mm rust metallic Czech glass smooth bicone beads
* **3** 9mm x 6mm violet Swarovski crystal teardrops
* **3** 8mm x 12mm Czech glass splatter finish green windowpane beads
* **3** 8mm x 12mm Czech glass splatter finish purple windowpane beads
* twisted sterling toggle clasp
* **3** khaki Swarovski chaton head pins
* **3** Balinese silver fancy head pins
* 22-gauge sterling head pin remnants (Did you save some head pin remnants like I asked you to? If not, use new head pins and cut off the heads. Then save the remnants for another project.)
* **2** 6mm sterling jump rings
* 6" (15cm) sterling figure 8 link chain

TOOLS

* snipe- or chain-nose pliers
* round-nose pliers
* flush cutters

PREPARE MATERIALS

REMOVE A 6" (15CM) SECTION OF PREMADE LINKED CHAIN AND LAY IT OUT ON YOUR WORK SURFACE ALONG WITH THE BEADS AND HEAD PINS NEEDED FOR THIS PIECE. GREEN WINDOWPANE OVALS AND VIOLET FACETED TEARDROPS GO ON "FANCY" HEAD PINS, AND THE REST OF THE BEADS GO ON PLAIN HEAD PINS.

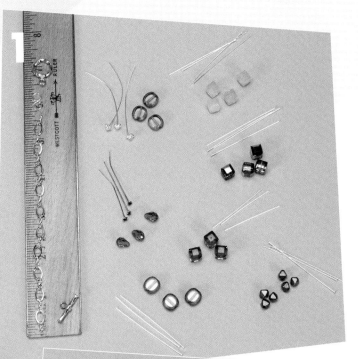

DESIGNER TIP

Each design in this book has endless variations. Every time you change up the beads, colors and materials, you create an entirely different mood. Don't get stuck in a rut...experiment!

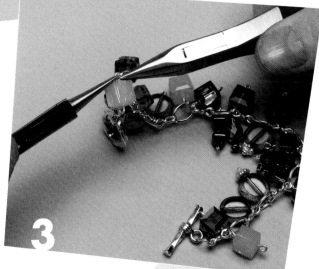

CREATE DANGLES

SLIDE THE VIOLET TEARDROPS ONTO CHATON HEAD PINS, AND SLIDE THE GREEN WINDOWPANE OVALS ONTO BALINESE SILVER HEAD PINS. SLIDE THE OTHER BEADS ONTO HEAD PIN REMNANTS (OR CUT THE HEADS OFF OF NEW HEAD PINS) AND MAKE A DECORATIVE LOOP WITH THE HEAD PIN WIRE AT THE BOTTOM OF THE BEAD. CUT THE HEAD PIN WIRE TO ³⁄₁₆" (5MM) ABOVE THE BEAD AND USE THE VERY TIP OF YOUR ROUND-NOSE PLIERS TO MAKE A VERY TINY LOOP AT THE TOP OF THE BEAD.

ATTACH CHARMS

ATTACH THE TOGGLES TO EITHER END OF THE STERLING SILVER CHAIN WITH 6MM JUMP RINGS. ATTACH THE DANGLES TO THE LINKED CHAIN BY LOOPING THE HEAD PIN WIRE AT THE TOP OF THE DANGLE AROUND THE LINKS. ATTACH THE DANGLES IN THE ORDER ILLUSTRATED IN THE DIAGRAM ON PAGE 60: A+B ON ONE LINK; C+D ON THE NEXT; AND E, F+G ON THE NEXT. REPEAT THE PATTERN UNTIL ALL OF THE DANGLES ARE ATTACHED.

quickie: DAINTY DEBUTANTE EARRINGS

Left over beads and head pins from the necklace accented with chain links have a coming out party as design elements in these "dainty Deb" earrings. How divine!

CISSY'S BY-THE-SEA
CHARM NECKLACE

IF YOU, TOO, DREAM OF SURF AND SAND AND WALKING THE BOARDS, AS WE SAY IN THE NORTHEAST, HERE IS A CHARM NECKLACE TO KEEP THE OCEAN WITH YOU ALL OF THE TIME.
Red, black and white were my grandmother's favorite colors and she also loved the beach, so this is my tribute to the incomparable Cis Scanlin... designed with love.

WHAT YOU WILL NEED

SUPPLIES
* small branch coral (center drilled)
* **8** 5mm white freshwater pearls
* **16** jet crystal Swarovski rounds
* **5** varied metal ocean-themed charms
* sterling hook and eye clasp
* **4** no. 4 crimp tubes
* **8** 24-gauge sterling head pins
* **5** 4mm sterling jump rings
* **2** 6" (15cm) lengths .030" (.76mm) 49 strand silver-plated wire

TOOLS
* mighty crimp tool
* round-nose pliers
* snipe-nose pliers
* chain-nose pliers
* ruler or bead board

RESOURCES: CORAL AND PEARLS FROM FIRE MOUNTAIN GEMS; CRYSTAL FROM SWAROVSKI; CHARMS FROM HIRSCHBERG SCHUTZ; STERLING FINDINGS FROM MARVIN SCHWAB; SILVER-PLATED WIRE AND LARGE CRIMPS FROM BEADALON

CONNECT FIRST BEAD SEGMENT TO SILVER-PLATED WIRE

PEARLS HAVE TEENIE, WEENIE, ITTY, BITTY, SQUITTY HOLES, SO THREAD THEM ON 24-GAUGE HEAD PINS. SLIDE ONE BLACK BEAD, ONE PEARL AND ANOTHER BLACK BEAD ONTO A HEAD PIN AND TURN A LOOP IN BOTH ENDS OF THE HEAD PIN. ATTACH A 6" (15CM) (4" [10CM] FINISHED LENGTH PLUS 2" [5CM] TO ALLOW FOR CRIMPING) PIECE OF SILVER-PLATED WIRE TO THE BLACK-AND-WHITE SEGMENT USING A NO. 4 CRIMP TUBE. IT IS IMPERATIVE THE WIRES DO NOT CROSS INSIDE THE CRIMP TUBE. USE THE MIGHTY CRIMP TOOL TO SMASH THE CRIMP TUBE. REPEAT FOR THE OTHER 6" (15CM) LENGTH OF SILVER-PLATED WIRE. (USE A RULER OR BEAD BOARD TO MEASURE THE WIRE PRIOR TO CRIMPING.)

PATIENCE BOOSTER

If you make all of your links first, you'll fly through the construction of a beaded chain.

BEGIN TO CREATE CHAIN

ATTACH A SECOND BLACK-AND-WHITE SEGMENT TO THE FIRST BLACK-AND-WHITE SEGMENT WITH A JUMP RING. CREATE THE CORAL SEGMENTS BY SLIDING NINE PIECES OF CORAL ONTO A HEAD PIN AND CREATING A LOOP ON EACH END OF THE HEAD PIN WITH ROUND-NOSE PLIERS. ATTACH THE LINKED BLACK-AND-WHITE SEGMENTS TO A CORAL SEGMENT. CONTINUE TO LINK THE BLACK-AND-WHITE PIECES TO THE RED CORAL PIECES IN THE FOLLOWING PATTERN: BLACK-AND-WHITE SEGMENT, JUMP RING, BLACK-AND-WHITE SEGMENT, CORAL SEGMENT. WHEN YOU FINISH THE CHAIN, YOU SHOULD HAVE USED EIGHT BLACK-AND-WHITE SEGMENTS AND FOUR RED CORAL SEGMENTS.

ATTACH CHARMS

ATTACH CLASPS TO THE SILVER-COATED WIRE USING NO. 4 CRIMP TUBES AND THE MIGHTY CRIMP TOOL. FINISH THE PIECE BY ATTACHING A CHARM TO EACH JUMP RING, WORKING FROM THE CENTER OUTWARDS UNTIL ALL FIVE CHARMS ARE PLACED. (BE SURE THAT EACH CHARM DANGLES FROM THE BOTTOM OF ITS JUMP RING.)

SWEETHEART
BIB NECKLACE

THIS DELICATE DESIGN IS THE POLAR OPPOSITE OF THE SOFT ROCK DIVA NECKLACE. For this piece you will be working on a micro scale. Truth be told, I ordered this chain thinking it was much larger, so imagine my surprise when it arrived and was so teeny-tiny. A happy accident! Remember that it is important to keep the scale and weight of your beads appropriate to the strength and look of your materials.

WHAT YOU WILL NEED

SUPPLIES
* **6** 4mm freshwater pearls
* **6** 4mm x 6mm small garnet teardrops
* **6** 3mm iolite rounds
* 19" (48cm) sterling cable fine 1.25mm chain (1 15" [38cm] length and 1 4" [10cm] length)
* sterling filigree locking clasp
* **18** 24-gauge sterling head pins
* **4** 4mm sterling jump rings

TOOLS
* round-nose pliers
* chain- or snipe-nose pliers
* flush cutters
* bead mat

SUPPLIERS: BEADS FROM THUNDERBIRD SUPPLY; STERLING HEAD PINS, CHAIN AND CLASP FROM JEWELRYSUPPLY.COM; TOOLS FROM EURO TOOL; BEAD MAT AND FLUSH CUTTERS FROM BEADALON

BEGIN TO CREATE DANGLES

CUT THE HEAD OFF OF A HEAD PIN AND THREAD IT THROUGH THE GARNET TEARDROP. BEND BOTH SIDES OF THE HEAD PIN UP INTO A "U" SHAPE. YOU CAN BEND THE HEAD PIN BY HAND BECAUSE STERLING SILVER WIRE IS EXTREMELY MALLEABLE.

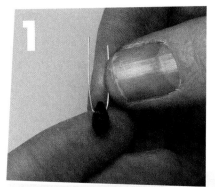

CONTINUE TO CREATE DANGLE

BEND ONE SIDE OF THE HEAD PIN WIRE BACK DOWN INTO AN UPSIDE DOWN "U" SHAPE.

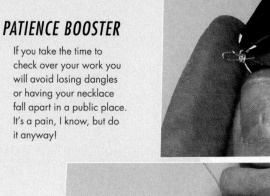

PATIENCE BOOSTER

If you take the time to check over your work you will avoid losing dangles or having your necklace fall apart in a public place. It's a pain, I know, but do it anyway!

CREATE WRAPPED LOOP

COIL THE STRAIGHT LEG OF THE HEAD PIN WIRE AROUND THE DOUBLED PIECE OF WIRE ON THE OTHER SIDE TO CREATE A COILED LOOP AT THE TOP OF THE BEAD. WRAP THE WIRE TIGHTLY AROUND AS MANY TIMES AS YOU CAN WITH YOUR FINGERS, AND FINISH WRAPPING WITH CHAIN-NOSE PLIERS. USE CHAIN-NOSE PLIERS TO TUCK IN THE END OF THE WIRE, AND THEN USE THOSE PLIERS AGAIN TO TURN THE LOOP SIDEWAYS SO IT WILL LAY FLAT AS IT HANGS FROM THE NECKLACE CHAIN. CLIP OFF ANY EXCESS WIRE TAIL WITH FLUSH CUTTERS.

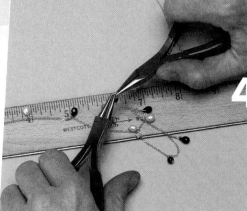

ATTACH DANGLES TO CHAIN

CREATE A TOTAL OF SIX GARNET DANGLES. MAKE SIX PEARL AND SIX IOLITE DANGLES BY THREADING THEM ON HEAD PINS AND CREATING A COILED LOOP ABOVE EACH BEAD. ATTACH THE CLASP TO THE ENDS OF THE CHAIN WITH 4MM JUMP RINGS. ATTACH THE DANGLES TO THE CHAIN AT ONE-INCH (5CM) INTERVALS WITH JUMP RINGS IN THE FOLLOWING SEQUENCE: IOLITE DANGLE, GARNET DANGLE, PEARL DANGLE. END WITH A PEARL DANGLE. USE JUMP RINGS TO ATTACH DANGLES TO THE 4" (10CM) CHAIN IN THE SAME PATTERN. ADD THE 4" (10CM) BEADED LENGTH OF CHAIN TO THE LONGER CHAIN AT THE SEVENTH BEAD FROM THE CLASP ON EACH SIDE USING JUMP RINGS AND PLIERS TO SECURE IT.

quickie: SWEETHEART EARRINGS

Make these super-simple linear earrings by combining a 2" (5cm) length of fine chain, a French ear wire and one of each bead left over from the necklace on a head pin. The result is a trés cool delicate drop earring. Repeat to finish the pair.

HAUTE HIPPIE
NECKLACE

SOMETIMES YOU FEEL LIKE A GLAMOUR PUSS, AND SOMETIMES YOU FEEL LIKE A NATURAL WOMAN—AND SOMETIMES YOU FEEL LIKE A NATURAL GLAMOUR PUSS.
You're a woman of many moods and many styles. That's part of the fun of being female—you can decide who you want to be each morning and accessorize accordingly! This lovely necklace features diffused earthy colors with the slightest hint of sparkle. Think of it as hippie haute couture.

SIZE 15 FOREST GREEN SEED BEAD

12MM x 7MM ROSE QUARTZ DIAMOND-SHAPED BEAD

6MM X 4MM FACETED AB SOFT GREEN CZECH GLASS DONUTS

6MM FACETED AB CZECH GLASS BROWN OVAL

3MM FACETED SOFT GREEN CZECH GLASS OVAL

10MM FACETED AVENTURINE COIN

WHAT YOU WILL NEED

SUPPLIES
* **8** 10mm faceted aventurine coins
* **9** 12mm x 7mm rose quartz diamond-shaped beads
* **16** 6mm faceted AB Czech glass brown ovals
* **34** 6mm x 4mm faceted AB soft green Czech glass donuts
* **8** 3mm faceted soft green Czech glass ovals
* **1** tube size 15 forest green seed beads
* sterling hook and eye clasp
* **8** 24-gauge sterling head pins
* **8** 4mm sterling jump rings
* **2** no. 2 sterling crimp tubes
* **22"** (56cm) .015" (.38mm) 19 or 49 strand wire

TOOLS
* short snipe-nose pliers or chain-nose pliers
* round-nose pliers
* oblique cutters or flush cutters
* crimp tool
* bead board

66

RESOURCES: CZECH GLASS FROM YORK NOVELTY; AVENTURINE COINS FROM GREAT CRAFT WORKS; ROSE QUARTZ DIAMONDS FROM PHOENIX JEWELRY AND PARTS; WIRE FROM BEADALON

MAKE DANGLES

ARRANGE ALL OF YOUR BEADS ON THE BEAD BOARD.
THREAD A 3MM GREEN CZECH OVAL BEAD AND A FACETED
AVENTURINE COIN ONTO A HEAD PIN. USE THE ROUND-
NOSE PLIERS TO HOLD THE WIRE STEADY AS YOU BEND THE
WIRE TO A 90° ANGLE WITH YOUR FINGER.

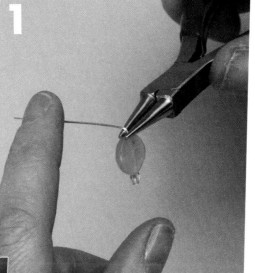

DESIGNER TIP

You might associate earth tones with
fall color palettes, but here the softer
greens, blush pinks and iridescent
browns give the design a spring time
feel. Just remember, the more you
explore color, the more interesting
your designs will be.

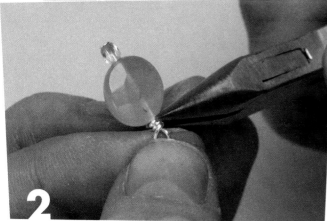

MAKE A WRAPPED LOOP

MAKE A WRAPPED LOOP WITH THE HEAD PIN WIRE BY
MOVING THE ROUND-NOSE PLIERS TO THE OTHER SIDE
OF THE BENT WIRE AND ROTATING THEM TOWARD
YOU TO CREATE A LOOP. WRAP THE REMAINDER OF
THE HEAD PIN WIRE AROUND THE BASE OF THE LOOP
AND TUCK THE REMAINING WIRE IN WITH THE SHORT
SNIPE-NOSE PLIERS. CREATE SEVEN MORE DANGLES.

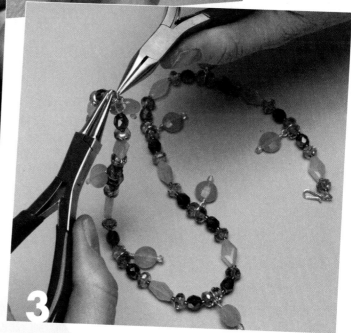

ATTACH CHARMS

CONSTRUCT THE CORE NECKLACE BY STRINGING THE BEADS ONTO THE
WIRE IN THE PATTERN AS SHOWN, BEGINNING WITH A SEED BEAD. CON-
TINUE BEADING IN THE ESTABLISHED PATTERN UNTIL YOU REACH THE END
OF THE NECKLACE. ATTACH THE DANGLES WITH 4MM JUMP RINGS,
INSERTING EACH JUMP RING BETWEEN TWO GREEN DONUT BEADS.
ATTACH THE REMAINING END OF THE CLASP WITH A CRIMP TUBE. SNIP
OFF THE WIRE TAIL WITH FLUSH CUTTERS.

VICTORIAN TEMPTRESS
CHOKER

NEED SOME SPARKLE TO JAZZ UP LAST YEAR'S LITTLE BLACK PARTY DRESS?

The budget-conscious among us know that when our wallets can't handle the cost of the latest fashions, our funds will cover a striking accessory that makes the old new again. This choker will surround your neck with a halo of sparkling color—it's perfect for the prom, your cousin Fran's wedding or a hot night in the big city. Wear this whenever you want to feel like the belle of the ball.

CRYSTAL
BUTTERFLY SLIDER

4MM FUCHSIA
SWAROVSKI BICONE

4MM TOURMALINE
SWAROVSKI BICONE

4MM KHAKI
SWAROVSKI BICONE

LIGHT ROSE
SUNFLOWER SLIDER

METAL LEAF
CHARM

RESOURCES: METAL MULTISTRAND SPACERS AND METAL LEAVES FROM BLUE MOON BEADS; CRYSTALS FROM SWAROVSKI; SLIDERS (FLOWER AND BUTTERFLY) FROM PURE ALLURE/CRYSTAL INNOVATIONS; WIRE, HOOK, HEAD PINS AND JUMP RINGS FROM BEADALON

WHAT YOU WILL NEED

SUPPLIES

* **11** light rose sunflower sliders
* **9** crystal butterfly sliders
* **11** small metal leaf charms
* **2** two-strand floral metal spacer beads
* **40** 4mm fuchsia Swarovski bicones
* **40** 4mm tourmaline Swarovski bicones
* **30** 4mm khaki Swarovski bicones
* sterling hook and eye clasp (hook only)
* approx. **34** 4mm jump rings
* **11** 22-gauge head or eye pins
* **4** no. 2 crimp tubes
* **2** 19" (48cm) lengths of .018" (.46mm) 7, 19 or 49 strand wire

TOOLS

* round-nose pliers
* short snipe-nose or chain-nose pliers
* oblique or flush cutters
* multichannel bead board

BEGIN DANGLES

CREATE DANGLES OUT OF THE SLIDER BEADS BY SLIDING A HEAD OR EYE PIN DIAGONALLY THROUGH TWO OF THE HOLES. CLIP OFF THE HEAD IF USING A HEAD PIN, OR USE AN EYE PIN. MAKE LOOPS IN BOTH ENDS OF THE WIRE WITH ROUND-NOSE PLIERS.

FINISH DANGLES

ATTACH A LEAF CHARM TO THE BOTTOM LOOP THAT YOU CREATED. THE LOOPS AT THE TOP AND BOTTOM OF THE FLOWERS SHOULD BE PERPENDICULAR TO ONE ANOTHER SO THAT THE LEAF CHARM LIES FLAT.

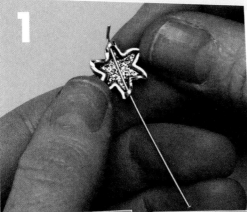

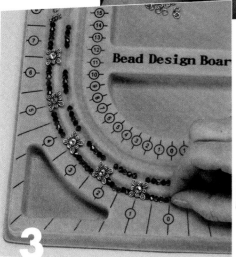

LAY OUT BEADS ON BEAD BOARD

ARRANGE ALL OF THE BEADS ON YOUR BEAD BOARD IN THE PATTERN AS SHOWN ABOVE, IN TWO SEPARATE CHANNELS. THE BOTTOM STRAND HAS ONE EXTRA KHAKI BEAD PER PATTERN SEGMENT SO THAT IT LAYS CORRECTLY. CRIMP TWO 19" (48CM) LENGTHS OF WIRE TO TWO JUMP RINGS. ATTACH THESE TWO JUMP RINGS TO A THIRD JUMP RING AND ATTACH THE FINAL JUMP RING TO THE STERLING HOOK CLASP END (FORMING A TRIANGLE SHAPE WHEN CONNECTED). STARTING WITH THE TWO-STRAND SPACER, STRING THE BEADS ONTO THE WIRE IN THE PATTERN AS SHOWN, STRINGING THE SLIDER BEADS ONTO BOTH STRANDS OF WIRE. YOU MAY ALSO STRING ON THE DANGLES AT THIS POINT, OR YOU MAY ADD THEM LATER BY OPENING AND CLOSING THE TOP LOOP ON EACH PIN TO LINK THEM SECURELY BETWEEN THE BEADS IN THE BOTTOM STRAND.

MAKE CHAIN WITH JUMP RINGS

ATTACH THE FREE END OF THE WIRES TO A JUMP RING. USE JUMP RINGS TO CREATE A HANDMADE CHAIN BY OPENING ONE RING, ATTACHING IT TO THE NEXT, AND CLOSING THE JUMP RING. CONTINUE TO OPEN THE NEXT JUMP RING AND ATTACH A JUMP RING UNTIL THE CHAIN IS THE LENGTH YOU DESIRE. (FITTED CHOKERS NEED EXTENSION CHAIN TO ALLOW FOR ADJUSTMENT TO YOUR SPECIFIC NECK SIZE.)

ADD CLASP

ATTACH A DANGLE TO THE END OF THE HANDMADE CHAIN.

PATIENCE BOOSTER

If you want to save time, use a pre-made chain here. I figured out when constructing this design that in order for it to fall properly when worn, the top row had to be slightly shorter than the bottom row...after stringing the entire piece... grrr...but my frustration paid off for you. You are welcome! Ha!

all tied up

This chapter introduces you to the wonderful world of creative cording. You'll use silk, leather, stretch cord and ribbon to create a multitude of textured, crimped and knotted designs. After you perfect these techniques, you will have opened up an entirely new world for yourself as a designer. Knot work can create all different kinds of effects. Knotting thick leather cord to station larger beads creates a chunky look, while knotting thin silk thread creates an elegant effect that works well with pearls or other more delicate beads. It's probably best to begin with a knotting project that uses larger cording and progress toward finer cord as your fingers grow ever more nimble.

"WHEN I'M INSPIRED, I GET EXCITED BECAUSE I CAN'T WAIT TO SEE WHAT I'LL COME UP WITH NEXT."
—DOLLY PARTON

TECHNIQUES

- **THE MIGHTY, MIGHTY CRIMP TOOL**
- **KNOT STATIONS**
- **ASYMMETRICAL DESIGN**
- **STRETCHY STUFF**
- **THE TRI-CORD KNOTTER**

GIRLY GOOD
BERRIES + BOWS PIN

I HAVE BEEN COLLECTING VINTAGE CLOTHING, ACCESSORIES AND KNICK-KNACKS FOR OVER TWENTY YEARS NOW.

In fact, there was even a time when I lived in vintage. Those days have passed, but I still love to throw a retro nod into my day-to-day wardrobe, and I am especially partial to cherries, berries and gingham. Imagine my delight when I ran across this adorable ribbon and let it spark a new design. Sometimes you have to leave the bead aisle if you want to get some fresh ideas!

WHAT YOU WILL NEED

SUPPLIES
* **2** peridot green Czech glass leaves
* **2** red AB Czech glass berry beads
* 8" (20cm) Jelly Plaid red ribbon, ⅝" (16mm) width
* SP pin/pendant component
* **8** 4mm SP jump rings
* 2" (5cm) 20-gauge green wire (Colourcraft)
* GS Hypo Cement

TOOLS
* sharp sewing scissors
* round-nose pliers
* snipe- or chain-nose pliers

RESOURCES: CZECH GLASS FROM YORK NOVELTY; PIN AND JUMP RINGS FROM JEWELRYSUPPLY.COM; RIBBON FROM OFFRAY; COLOURCRAFT WIRE AND GS HYPO CEMENT FROM BEADALON

THREAD RIBBON ONTO PIN

THREAD APPROXIMATELY 8" (20CM) OF RIBBON THROUGH THE TWO HOLES IN THE PIN FORM, THREADING THEM THROUGH FROM THE BACK TO THE FRONT.

SECURE ENDS OF RIBBON

TIE A BOW WITH THE RIBBON AND TRIM THE ENDS. DAB A LINE OF GS HYPO CEMENT ON THE CUT EDGES OF THE RIBBON TO PREVENT FRAYING. ALLOW THE GS TO DRY. TRIM AWAY ANY FRAYED ENDS.

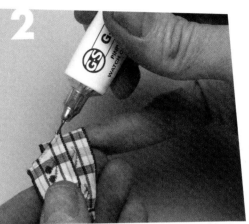

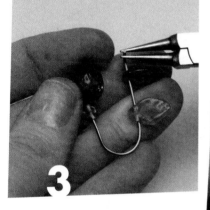

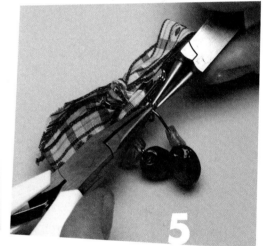

MAKE CHERRY CHARM

THREAD ONE BERRY BEAD ONTO A 2" (5CM) LENGTH OF GREEN 20-GAUGE COLOURCRAFT WIRE. MAKE A TINY LOOP WITH YOUR ROUND-NOSE PLIERS ON THE BACK SIDE OF THE BEAD (THE SIDE WITHOUT THE IRIDESCENT AB SHINE) TO SECURE IT. SLIDE ON A LEAF, BEND THE WIRE INTO A "U" SHAPE, SLIDE ON ANOTHER LEAF AND THEN SLIDE ON ANOTHER BERRY BEAD, MAKING SURE THAT THE SHINY SIDE (THE AB FINISH SIDE) IS FACING FRONT. TRIM THE WIRE SO THAT IT'S ABOUT 1½" (4CM) LONG. MAKE A LOOP BEHIND THE OTHER BERRY BEAD WITH THE ROUND-NOSE PLIERS.

MAKE JUMP RING CHAIN

ATTACH ONE JUMP RING TO EACH HOLE IN THE PIN FORM USING YOUR ROUND-NOSE AND CHAIN-NOSE PLIERS. LINK TWO JUMP RINGS TO EACH OF THOSE TWO JUMP RINGS. LINK THE TWO SEPARATE "MINI CHAINS" TOGETHER WITH ANOTHER JUMP RING. ATTACH ONE MORE JUMP RING TO THE JUMP RING THAT JOINS THE TWO SMALL CHAINS FOR A TOTAL OF EIGHT JUMP RINGS.

ATTACH BERRY CHARM

ATTACH THE BERRY CHARM TO THE FINAL JUMP RING IN THE CHAIN.

DESIGNER TIP

I love to rummage around all kinds of stores for unique new items to add to my bag of tricks. You never know what you might find in a craft store, sewing store, thrift shop, hardware store… keep your design antennae working everywhere you go!

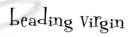

METROSEXUAL
BRACELET

DOES YOUR GUY HOG THE MIRROR, THE HAIR PRODUCTS AND THE SKIN CREAM?

Does he sneak off for pedicures during his lunch breaks? Do you find yourself waiting for him to get ready so you two can hit the town? Why should girls have all of the fun? Surprise your metrosexual man (or dare we say "girly man" ha) with this leather and metal bracelet, and see if he is man enough to sport it around town!

WHAT YOU WILL NEED

SUPPLIES
* **6** metal freckle beads
* **6** metal spiral beads
* textured large toggle clasp
* **30** no. 4 crimp tubes
* **3** 10" (25cm) lengths of size 1.5mm black leather cord

TOOLS
* mighty crimp tool
* flush cutters
* ruler or bead board

RESOURCES: METAL BEADS FROM BLUE MOON BEADS; TOGGLE CLASP FROM HALCRAFT BEAD HEAVEN; LEATHER AND CRIMP TUBES FROM BEADALON

ATTACH LEATHER TO CLASP

ARRANGE THE THREE 10" (25CM) STRANDS OF BLACK LEATHER CORD (8½" [22CM] FINISHED LENGTH PLUS 1½" [6CM] EXTRA FOR ATTACHING TO CLASP) ON YOUR WORK SURFACE. THREAD A NO. 4 CRIMP TUBE ONTO ONE CORD AND THREAD THE CORD THROUGH THE CLASP AND BACK THROUGH THE CRIMP TUBE. FLATTEN THE CRIMP TUBE WITH THE MIGHTY CRIMP TOOL. REPEAT WITH THE OTHER STRANDS, SECURING THEM ALL TO ONE END OF THE CLASP. TRIM AWAY ANY EXCESS LEATHER TAIL.

THREAD ON FIRST CRIMP TUBE

LAY THE LEATHER STRANDS ON THE TABLE NEXT TO A RULER. MEASURE 1" (3CM) FROM THE CLASP AND THREAD A NO. 4 CRIMP TUBE ONTO ONE OF THE STRANDS. SECURE THE CRIMP TUBE WITH THE MIGHTY CRIMPER.

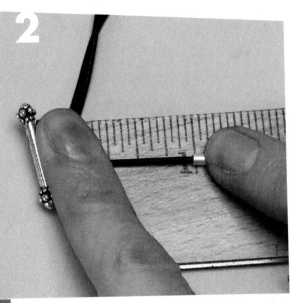

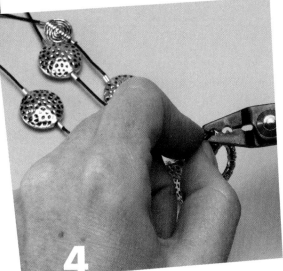

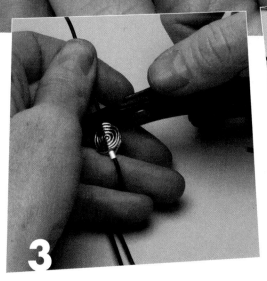

SECURE FIRST BEAD

SLIDE ON A SILVER BEAD AND THEN ANOTHER CRIMP TUBE. FLATTEN THAT CRIMP TUBE TO STATION THE BEAD.

FINISH BRACELET

BEAD THE THREE LEATHER STRANDS, SPACING THE BEADS ON EACH STRAND AT SLIGHTLY DIFFERENT INTER-VALS. WHEN ALL THREE STRANDS ARE BEADED, ATTACH THEM TO THE OTHER SIDE OF THE CLASP, USING A NO. 4 CRIMP TUBE FOR EACH STRAND.

DESIGNER TIP

If the crimp spacing technique isn't your cup of tea, use a heavier diameter of leather and knot the beads into place. Don't stress if the spacing isn't perfect, unless you can't help yourself, in which case you are probably reading the wrong book!

KNICKERS IN KNOTS
NECKLACE

**THESE LOVELY LITTLE TRANSLU-
CENT BEADS COME FROM
INDONESIA IN AN ARRAY OF
WATERCOLOR SHADES.**
They are so lightweight that you can
pile them on and still have a design
that is as light as air. Here I have
combined them with natural leather
for a fun and easy project you can
whip up at a moment's notice.

WHAT YOU WILL NEED

SUPPLIES

* **4** 19mm x 19mm cantaloupe diamond resin beads
* **3** 12mm x 10mm kiwi flat oval resin beads
* **3** 28mm x 16mm light pink oval slice resin beads
* **4** 13mm x 13mm lemon diamond resin beads
* sterling silver toggle clasp
* **6** SP fold-over ends
* **5** 4mm jump rings
* **3** 20" (51cm) lengths of 1.5mm natural leather cord

TOOLS

* oblique or flush cutters
* chain-nose pliers
* bead mat or bead board
* your nimble fingers

RESOURCES: LUCITE BEADS FROM NATURAL TOUCH; RESIN
BEADS, LEATHER, JUMP RINGS AND CORD ENDS FROM
BEADALON; CLASP FROM MARVIN SCHWAB

ATTACH FOLD-OVER ENDS TO LEATHER STRANDS

PUT THE VERY END OF ONE 20" (51CM) STRAND OF LEATHER CORDING INTO THE METAL FOLD-OVER END AND USE THE CHAIN-NOSE PLIERS TO SMASH DOWN ONE SIDE OF THE FOLD-OVER END, WRAPPING IT AROUND THE LEATHER. REPEAT FOR THE OTHER "ARM" OF THE FOLD-OVER END. CONTINUE ATTACH-ING THE FOLD-OVER ENDS TO ONE END OF EACH OF THE THREE STRANDS OF LEATHER.

KNOT LEATHER

MEASURE 2½" (6CM) FROM THE FOLD-OVER END AND MARK IT WITH YOUR THUMB AS YOU TIE AN OVERHAND KNOT AT THAT SPOT. WHILE TIGHTENING THE KNOT, MAKE SURE TO KEEP YOUR THUMB AT THE 2½" (6CM) MARK SO THAT THE KNOT ENDS UP IN THE CORRECT SPOT.

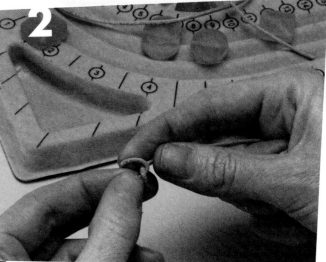

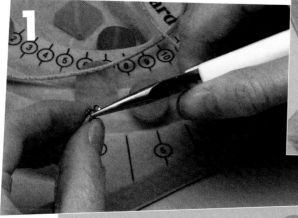

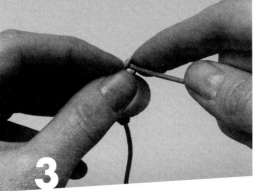

SECURE FIRST BEAD

SLIDE A LIGHT PINK BEAD ONTO ONE OF THE LEATHER STRANDS AND MAKE ANOTHER OVERHAND KNOT FLUSH WITH THE EDGE OF THE BEAD TO SECURE IT. HOLDING THE BEAD STEADY, USE YOUR POINTER FINGERS TO EXERT AN EVEN PRESSURE ON THE KNOT AS YOU TIGHTEN IT SO THAT IT RESTS FLUSH AGAINST THE EDGE OF THE BEAD. MEASURE 1½" (4CM) FROM THE LAST KNOT AND CONTINUE KNOT-TING THE BEADS IN THE FOLLOWING SEQUENCE: CAN-TALOUPE, KIWI, LEMON, LIGHT PINK. REPEAT FOR A SECOND STRAND IN THE FOLLOWING SEQUENCE: LEMON, KIWI, CANTALOUPE, LIGHT PINK, LEMON. REPEAT FOR THE THIRD STRAND IN THE FOLLOWING SEQUENCE: CANTALOUPE, LEMON, LIGHT PINK, KIWI, CANTALOUPE. (YOU CAN OPT TO SPACE THE BEADS RANDOMLY TO CREATE A NECKLACE WITH A DIFFERENT LOOK, IF YOU SO DESIRE.)

ATTACH CLASP

ATTACH FOLD-OVER ENDS TO THE ENDS OF THE LEATHER STRANDS. ATTACH TWO CONNECTED JUMP RINGS TO THE CIRCLE END OF THE TOGGLE, AND ADD IT TO THE FOLD-OVER END. FINALLY, ADD A CHAIN OF THREE 4MM CONNECTED JUMP RINGS TO THE END, FOLLOWED BY THE BAR END OF THE TOGGLE CLASP.

DESIGNER TIP

You can use this hand knotting tech-nique with leather, suede, rattail cord, hemp, yarn...any large diameter stringing medium you choose. These beads look terrific on funky yarn; just use a flexible bead needle to thread it through the beads.

NATURE GIRL
BRACELET

THESE JASPER STONES IN THEIR VARIEGATED COLORS REMIND ME OF A SOUTH-WESTERN SUNSET OVER A DESERT CANYON...

well...I have never actually seen a Southwestern sunset over a desert canyon...but this is how I think one would look. No two pieces of jasper will ever be exactly the same, which means you will have your own unique bracelet! Natural gemstones can vary widely from stone to stone in appearance. Choose the individual beads that suit you best to make your one-of-a-kind bracelet.

WHAT YOU WILL NEED

SUPPLIES
* **1** 38mm x 20mm two-hole brecciated jasper station bead
* **2** 10mm x 14mm brecciated jasper flat oval beads
* **3** 5mm x 7mm rainbow jasper hexagon beads
* **2** 8mm x 12mm green jasper rectangles
* small SP toggle clasp
* **4** gunmetal eye pins
* **14** 3mm gunmetal jump rings
* 8mm silver jump ring
* 12" (30cm) 1mm black leather cord

TOOLS
* round-nose pliers
* short snipe- or chain-nose pliers
* oblique or flush cutters
* bead mat

RESOURCES: BEADS FROM THUNDERBIRD SUPPLY; LEATHER AND CLASP FROM BEADALON; JASPER BRACELET 2-HOLE BEAD FROM FIRE MOUNTAIN GEMS; GUNMETAL JUMP RINGS FROM RINGS AND THINGS

KNOT CENTER BEAD

SLIDE THE LARGE TWO-HOLE JASPER BEAD ONTO THE CENTER OF A 12" (30CM) LENGTH OF BLACK LEATHER CORD. TIE A DOUBLE KNOT TO SECURE THE STONE.

DESIGNER TIP

This design came from letting the beads guide me. They spoke to me...okay, not really because that would be freaky...but they did seem to know where they wanted to go and I tried to take them there! Erase your mind and follow the beads.

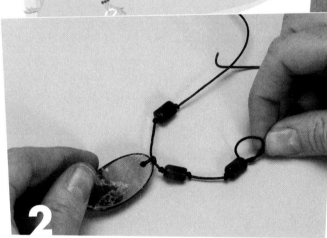

TIE ON RED JASPER BEADS

TIE A KNOT IN ONE STRAND OF THE LEATHER CORD, LEAVING A SMALL SPACE AFTER THE JASPER STONE. SLIDE ON A RECTANGULAR RED JASPER BEAD (RAINBOW JASPER HEXAGON) AND TIE ANOTHER KNOT FLUSH AGAINST THE BEAD TO SECURE IT ON THE LEATHER. TIE ON ANOTHER RED JASPER BEAD, A LITTLE FARTHER UP THE LEATHER CORD. TIE THE REMAINING RECTANGULAR BEAD ASYMMETRICALLY ONTO THE OTHER STRAND OF LEATHER CORD.

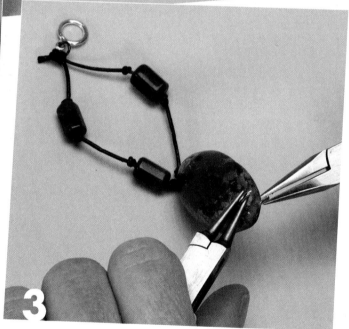

ADD CLASP, LINK JUMP RING TO JASPER STONE

INSERT A GUNMETAL JUMP RING INTO THE CIRCLE PIECE OF THE TOGGLE CLASP. TIE A ROUGH KNOT WITH THE TWO STRANDS OF LEATHER CORD AROUND THE JUMP RING. CUT THE LEATHER TAIL, LEAVING A LITTLE SHOWING. INSERT A GUNMETAL JUMP RING INTO THE OPEN HOLE ON THE OTHER SIDE OF THE LARGE JASPER STONE.

CONSTRUCT CHAIN SIDE OF BRACELET

ATTACH A CHAIN OF TWO 3MM GUNMETAL JUMP RINGS TO THE LARGE METAL JUMP RING. SLIDE A FLAT OVAL JASPER BEAD ONTO A GUNMETAL EYE PIN, CUT THE EYE PIN ABOVE THE BEAD WITH FLUSH CUTTERS, AND TURN A LOOP WITH ROUND-NOSE PLIERS. REPEAT WITH A GREEN JASPER RECTANGLE. ATTACH THE TWO BEADED EYE PINS TO THE FIRST JUMP RINGS IN THE CHAIN WITH TWO MORE GUNMETAL JUMP RINGS.

PATIENCE BOOSTER

Many gemstones are hand-drilled, and therefore their holes can vary in diameter. This is where your handy dandy bead reamer comes to save the day! You can save yourself a little time and a little stress by being proactive—go ahead and ream all of the beads you're planning to use for the piece before you begin. Then you won't have to interrupt the beading flow. Ohm.

FINISH BRACELET

CONTINUE TO LINK THE BEADS IN THE PATTERN AS SHOWN (ON OVAL BEAD SIDE: TWO JUMP RINGS, ANOTHER OVAL BEAD; ON RECTANGLE BEAD SIDE: THREE JUMP RINGS, ANOTHER RECTANGLE BEAD). ADD ONE MORE JUMP RING TO EACH BEADED CHAIN AND LINK THE TWO CHAINS TOGETHER WITH ANOTHER JUMP RING. ADD TWO MORE JUMP RINGS AND ATTACH THE BAR END OF THE TOGGLE CLASP TO THE FINAL JUMP RING.

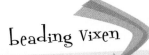

GARDEN NYMPH
CRYSTAL STRETCH BRACELETS

THE ONLY ADJECTIVE THAT FULLY DESCRIBES THESE DELIGHTFUL BRACELETS IS "SPARKLETASTIC."
Okay, technically it isn't a word... but who cares! To help you see how much color can change the look of a piece, I have created three color palettes with the same design so you can pick the one that suits you best. This looks really complicated, but it isn't. Wrap your wrist in sparkly goodness!

4MM VIOLET SWAROVSKI BICONE

4MM X 6MM VIOLET OPAL SWAROVSKI DONUT

4MM KHAKI SWAROVSKI BICONE

3MM VITRIAL MEDIUM SWAROVSKI ROUNDS

8MM TANZANITE SWAROVSKI CENTER-DRILLED FLOWER

WHAT YOU WILL NEED

SUPPLIES
* **8** 8mm tanzanite Swarovski center-drilled flowers
* **7** 4mm x 6mm violet opal Swarovski donuts
* **28** 4mm violet Swarovski bicones
* **28** 4mm khaki Swarovski bicones
* **28** 3mm vitrial medium Swarovski rounds
* **7** ball-tipped sterling head pins
* 22" (56cm) elonga or fibrous flat stretch cord
* GS Hypo Cement

TOOLS
* round-nose pliers
* snipe- or chain-nose pliers
* flush cutters
* bead board

RESOURCES: CRYSTAL FROM SWAROVSKI; HEAD PINS FROM MARVIN SCHWAB; ELONGA STRETCH CORD FROM BEADALON

81

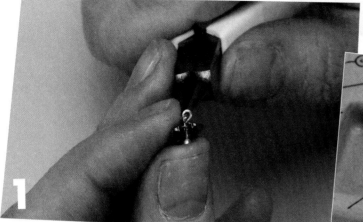

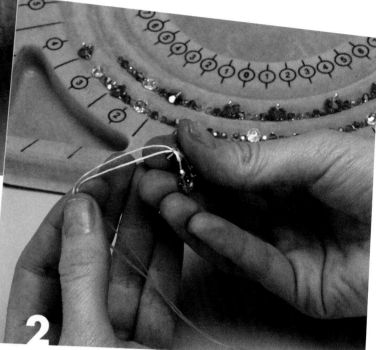

MAKE MINI "DANGLES"

SLIDE A PURPLE TANZANITE FLOWER ONTO A BALL-TIPPED HEAD PIN, BEND THE WIRE FLUSH TO THE UNDERSIDE OF THE FLOWER, AND USE FLUSH CUTTERS TO CUT THE WIRE DOWN TO ³⁄₁₆" (5MM) ABOVE THE BEAD. USE THE TIP OF THE ROUND-NOSE PLIERS TO MAKE A SMALL LOOP IN THE HEAD PIN WIRE. REPEAT FOR THE SEVEN REMAINING TANZANITE FLOWERS.

DESIGNER TIP

I gave you three color palettes to show you how a design changes when you change the colors. Each palette is basically three colors— now test your design skills and see if you can come up with a fourth palette…ready, set, go!

MAKE LOOP CLOSURE

ONCE YOU HAVE ALL OF THE FLOWER DANGLES MADE, LAY OUT THE BEADS ON YOUR BEAD BOARD IN THE PATTERN AS SHOWN IN THE DIAGRAM ON PAGE 81. FOLD THE 22" (56CM) OF ELASTIC CORDING IN HALF. TO CREATE THE LOOP CLOSURE, THREAD ON SIX BEADS: TWO VIOLET CRYSTALS, TWO KHAKI CRYSTALS AND TWO VITRIAL CRYSTALS, SO THAT THERE IS ONE BEAD OF EACH COLOR ON EACH SIDE OF THE LOOP IN THE CORDING. THREAD BOTH STRANDS THROUGH THE LOOP OF A PURPLE FLOWER DANGLE.

BEGIN STRINGING BEADS

BEGIN BEADING THE BRACELET IN THE PATTERN AS SHOWN IN THE DIAGRAM ON PAGE 81, BEGINNING WITH TWO VITRIAL ROUNDS, ONE ON EACH STRAND. WHEN YOU HAVE STRUNG THREE BEADS ONTO EACH STRAND, THEN THREAD BOTH STRANDS TOGETHER THROUGH A DONUT BEAD. COMPLETE THE FIRST CYCLE OF THE PATTERN AND CONTINUE BEADING.

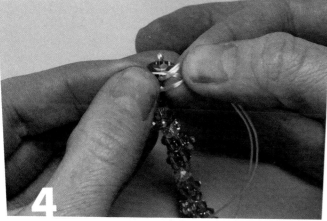

TIE OFF END OF BRACELET

FINISH BEADING THE BRACELET IN THE ESTABLISHED PATTERN. THREAD THE FINAL PURPLE FLOWER DANGLE BEAD ONTO ONE STRAND OF ELASTIC. TIE THE TWO STRANDS TOGETHER, TIGHTENING THE BEADS. TIE AN OVERHAND KNOT WITH THE TWO STRANDS OF ELASTIC TO SECURE THE KNOT.

SECURE KNOT

APPLY A DAB OF GS HYPO CEMENT TO THE KNOT TO SECURE IT. LET THE GLUE DRY. TRIM THE ENDS OF THE ELASTIC CORDING. TO FASTEN THE BRACELET, SIMPLY SLIDE THE FINAL PURPLE DANGLE FLOWER THROUGH THE LOOP IN THE OTHER END OF THE BRACELET.

quickie: COLOR VARIATIONS

BEADS FOR PINK + GREY BRACELET

* ✻ **8** 8mm crystal AB Swarovski center-drilled flowers
* ✻ **7** 4mm x 6mm crystal AB Swarovski donuts
* ✻ **28** 4mm black diamond Swarovski bicones
* ✻ **28** 4mm hyacinth Swarovski bicones
* ✻ **28** 3mm jet Swarovski rounds

BEADS FOR RED + BLACK BRACELET

* ✻ **8** light rose Swarovski center-drilled flowers
* ✻ **7** 4mm x 6mm crystal AB Swarovski donuts
* ✻ **28** 4mm Indian sapphire Swarovski bicones
* ✻ **28** 4mm black diamond Swarovski bicones
* ✻ **28** 3mm light rose AB Swarovski rounds

beading goddess

BETTY RUBBLE-INSPIRED
CRYSTAL PEARL NECKLACE

THESE BOLD AUTUMNAL-TONED SWAROVSKI PEARLS ARE KNOTTED ON SILK TO CREATE A CLASSIC NECKLACE PERFECT FOR WHEN YOU ARE FEELING ALL GROWN UP.

I love big, fat pearls...the bigger, the better! Real pearls this size would be worth a king's ransom, but these faux pearls have the weight and iridescence of the real thing—and at a fraction of the cost. Afraid of attempting knot work? You can always cheat and space the beads with small seed beads on wire, I won't tell! Better yet, roll up those sleeves and try something new.

WHAT YOU WILL NEED

SUPPLIES
* **10** 10mm black Swarovski crystal pearls
* **9** 10mm bronze Swarovski crystal pearls
* **9** 10mm light green Swarovski crystal pearls
* gold-plated magnetic clasp
* **2** gold-plated clamshells
* **1** package brown size 8 Perlside Griffin silk (with pre-attached needle)
* GS Hypo Cement

TOOLS
* Tri-Cord Knotter
* sharp scissors
* bead board
* short snipe- or chain-nose pliers
* round-nose pliers

RESOURCES: CRYSTAL PEARLS FROM SWAROVSKI; SILK, FINDINGS AND TRI-CORD KNOTTER FROM BEADALON

SLIDE ON CLAMSHELL

THREAD ONE GOLD CLAMSHELL ONTO THE UNCUT, FULL LENGTH OF SILK CORD. TIE A SIMPLE OVERHAND KNOT IN THE BEGINNING OF THE SILK CORD. SLIDE THE CLAMSHELL OVER THE KNOT SO THAT THE CLAMSHELL "SWALLOWS" THE KNOT AND CLOSES OVER IT. FLATTEN THE CLAMSHELL AROUND THE KNOT USING PLIERS (SEE STEP 9).

SECURE CLAM SHELL

TIE ANOTHER OVERHAND KNOT DIRECTLY AFTER THE CLAMSHELL AND USE YOUR THUMB AND FOREFINGER TO NESTLE THE KNOT FLUSH AGAINST THE CLAMSHELL.

STRING ON PEARLS

THREAD ON THE CRYSTAL PEARLS IN THE FOLLOWING PATTERN: BLACK, BRONZE, GREEN. REPEAT THE PATTERN UNTIL ALL OF THE PEARLS ARE STRUNG ONTO THE THREAD.

PATIENCE BOOSTER

The first few attempts at knotting are bound to make you a little crazy. Persevere, my dear. Even the technically challenged can master this skill. Make sure your cord is the right size for the holes in your beads or you will have to double up on knots. And consider buying a couple packages of silk cord—just in case the unthinkable happens (don't worry, it probably will…).

POSITION FINGERS FOR KNOTTING

BEGIN TO KNOT THE BEADS BY WRAPPING THE CORD AROUND YOUR INDEX AND MIDDLE FINGERS, AND THEN WRAP THE CORD AROUND THE BACK OF YOUR HAND AND IN FRONT OF YOUR RING FINGER. AS YOU CONTINUE TO WRAP, BRING THE KNOTTED CLAMSHELL END THROUGH THE SPACE CREATED BETWEEN YOUR MIDDLE AND RING FINGERS.

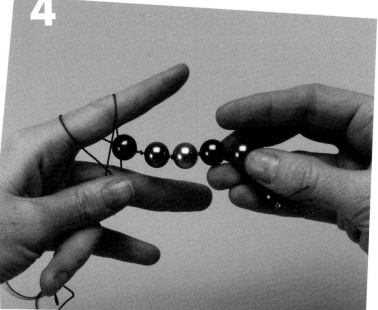

INSERT TRI-CORD KNOTTER

INSERT THE POINTED END OF THE TRI-CORD KNOTTER INTO THE KNOT THAT'S BEING CREATED, RIGHT AT THE "CRISS-CROSS" OF THE CORD, MAKING SURE THAT THE KNOTTER IS POINTING AND MOVING TO THE RIGHT.

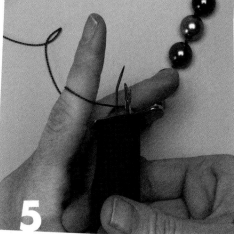

TIGHTEN KNOT WITH TRI-CORD KNOTTER

SLIDE THE KNOT ON THE TRI-CORD KNOTTER TOWARD THE CLAMSHELL END, TIGHTENING THE KNOT FLUSH AGAINST THE LAST PEARL.

SECURE CLAM SHELL AT END

WHEN YOU'VE KNOTTED THE WHOLE STRAND, THREAD ON THE CLAMSHELL. SPLIT THE SILK CORD EVENLY IN TWO AND TIE A DOUBLE KNOT WITH THE TWO SEPARATED STRANDS. DAB GS HYPO CEMENT ONTO THE KNOT AND ALLOW IT TO DRY.

SLIDE KNOT OFF TRI-CORD KNOTTER

RAISE THE "LEVER" OF THE TRI-CORD KNOTTER AND SLIP THE KNOT OFF OF THE TOOL SO THAT IT RESTS FLUSH AGAINST THE PEARL.

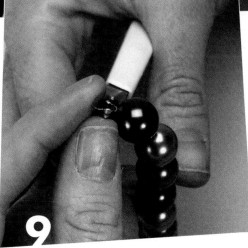

FLATTEN CLAMSHELL

FLATTEN THE CLAMSHELL OVER THE KNOT USING CHAIN-NOSE PLIERS SO THAT THE KNOT IS INSIDE THE CLAMSHELL.

ATTACH CLASP

ATTACH THE MAGNETIC CLASP TO THE LOOPS AT THE TOP OF YOUR CLAMSHELL USING YOUR PLIERS TO SECURE THEM CLOSED. ATTACH THE OTHER END OF THE CLASP TO THE CLAMSHELL AT THE BEGINNING OF THE NECKLACE.

heavy metal

FILL YOUR BIG BAG OF BEAD TRICKS WITH SOME SPARKLE AND SHINE. THIS IS A CHAPTER DEDICATED TO WIRE, CHAIN, HEAD PINS AND CHANNELS FOR THE MODERN GIRL WITH AN EDGE. WELCOME TO FUNKYTOWN, WHERE YOU ARE MISTRESS OF THE BEAD!

In this chapter, the focus is on integrating metal elements into your designs. Metal can be chunky and heavy, or it can be delicate and light. Depending on the color and size of the metal or chain you choose, you can pair it with a myriad of different beads and cords. The projects in this chapter couple metal and chain with everything from black leather cord and large beads to sparkling dangles made of Swarovski crystals and even a dragonfly made from beaded copper wire. You'll learn an amazing array of wire and chain techniques that will help you build and grow your skills. Dip your toes into the pool here for another exciting approach to creating beautiful jewelry that is sure to make a splash.

"IF I'D OBSERVED ALL THE RULES,
I'D NEVER HAVE GOTTEN ANYWHERE."
—MARILYN MONROE

TECHNIQUES

- THINKING BEYOND THE BEAD
- JUMP RING CONNECTORS
- USING PREMADE CHAIN
- THE BEADED BUG
- MULTI-DANGLE WATERFALL EFFECTS

DICHROIC
NECKLACE

DICHROIC GLASS IS A HANDCRAFTED MATERIAL THAT HAS AMAZING SHINE AND IRIDESCENCE; I LOVE TO COMBINE IT WITH METAL TO GET A VERY INDUSTRIAL LOOK. Designer Paula Radke has figured out how to mass produce this glass to make it affordable for all, yeah! This clean design will give a modern edge to your wardrobe...and the fun colors will punch up a basic black business suit.

12MM x 5MM PINK, SILVER AND BLACK STRIPED DICHROIC RECTANGLE BEAD

METAL BALLOON-SHAPED BEAD

14MM SILVER AND BLACK ROUND BEAD

METAL PUFF SQUARE BEAD

7MM x 7MM PINK, SILVER AND BLACK CUBE BEAD

5MM SILVER AND BLACK DONUT BEAD

WHAT YOU WILL NEED

SUPPLIES
* **5** 12mm x 5mm pink, silver and black striped dichroic rectangle beads
* **4** 7mm x 7mm pink, silver and black cube beads
* **8** 5mm silver and black donut beads
* **4** 14mm silver and black round beads
* **8** metal puff square beads
* **8** metal balloon-shaped beads
* square-center silver toggle clasp
* **21** silver eye pins
* **4**mm jump ring

TOOLS
* short snipe- or chain-nose pliers
* round-nose pliers
* oblique or flush cutters
* bead mat

RESOURCES: DICHROIC BEADS FROM PAULA RADKE; METAL BEADS AND TOGGLE CLASP FROM BLUE MOON BEADS; HEAD PINS FROM BEADALON; VARIATION CHAIN AND EARRING FINDINGS FROM FIRE MOUNTAIN GEMS

BUILD BEADED LINKS

BUILD THE SEPARATE LINKS IN THE CHAIN BY SLIDING SINGLE BEADS AND COMBINATIONS OF BEADS ONTO EYE PINS AS SHOWN IN THE DIAGRAM. BUILD THE LINKS BY SLIDING EACH BEAD OR COMBINATION OF BEADS ONTO AN EYE PIN AND ADDING A LOOP AT THE OTHER END USING ROUND-NOSE PLIERS (SEE TECHNIQUES, PAGE 16).

BUILD CHAIN

CONNECT A 4MM JUMP RING TO THE BAR END OF THE TOGGLE. LINK THE FIRST BEADED LINK TO THE JUMP RING AND CONTINUE TO BUILD THE CHAIN IN THE PATTERN AS SHOWN.

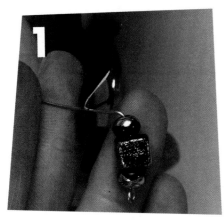

FINISH NECKLACE

FINISH THE NECKLACE BY ATTACHING THE SQUARE END OF THE TOGGLE CLASP TO THE FINAL LINK IN THE CHAIN.

DESIGNER TIP

Try combining dichroic glass with other materials to get a totally different look. I highly recommend throwing the rules away and experimenting. You won't always come out with a winning result, but this is how you begin to define your own design aesthetic.

quickie: DICHROIC NECKLACE + EARRINGS SET

Here are two more takes on the same idea—the flat shapes seemed to be begging to be grouped together for a swingy geometric pendant. Premade chain and funky earring wires lend an industrial feel. You can pump this design out in a hot second.

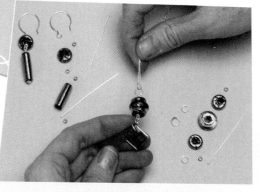

TO MAKE THIS NECKLACE, SIMPLY LINK THE DICHROIC BEADS OF YOUR CHOICE TOGETHER WITH HEAD PINS AND JUMP RINGS AND ATTACH THE RESULTING DANGLE TO A LARGER JUMP RING. SLIDE THE PENDANT ONTO A SIMPLE SILVER CHAIN TO FINISH. TO MAKE THE EARRINGS, SIMPLY SLIDE A LONG BEAD AND A SILVER SEED BEAD ONTO A HEAD PIN. LINK ANOTHER BEADED HEAD PIN TO THE FIRST AND ATTACH THE DANGLE TO AN EAR WIRE TO FINISH.

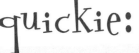

beading virgin

CASINO ROYALE
COLLAR

THESE SUPER SPARKLY SEW-ON STONES MADE BY SWAROVSKI ARE REALLY USED FOR ICE SKATING COSTUMES AND ELVIS IMPERSONATORS.
But when I saw them, I knew they were destined for better things than simply dangling from the skirt of a skater's leotard. Connected with jump rings, they make a necklace fit for a gangster's moll...if you don't know what a "moll" is, feel free to look it up. Paging Jean Harlow!

12MM CRYSTAL DORADO FOIL SEW-ON STONE

13MM X 18MM JET BLACK SEW-ON STONE

13MM X 18MM FOILED AB CRYSTAL SEW-ON STONE

WHAT YOU WILL NEED

SUPPLIES
* **7** 13mm x 18mm jet black sew-on stones
* **6** 13mm x 18mm foiled AB crystal sew-on stones
* **12** 12mm crystal dorado foil sew-on stones
* gold-plated large toggle clasp
* **28** 4mm gunmetal jump rings

TOOLS
* short snipe- or chain-nose pliers
* round-nose pliers
* bead board or bead mat

RESOURCES: SEW-ON STONES FROM SWAROVSKI; GUN-METAL JUMP RINGS FROM RINGS AND THINGS; TOGGLE CLASP FROM BEADALON

ATTACH TOGGLE

LAY OUT ALL OF THE SEW-ON STONES ON YOUR BEAD BOARD IN THE PATTERN AS SHOWN, BEGINNING WITH A CRYSTAL DORADO FOIL STONE. ATTACH THE BAR END OF THE TOGGLE CLASP TO THE FIRST STONE WITH A 4MM GUNMETAL JUMP RING USING THE ROUND-NOSE AND SHORT SNIPE-NOSE PLIERS TO OPEN AND CLOSE THE JUMP RING.

DESIGNER TIP

Here is another example of "thinking beyond the bead:" great ideas often come from the most unexpected places. There are tons of cool items to integrate into your beadwork at your local sewing and hardware stores.

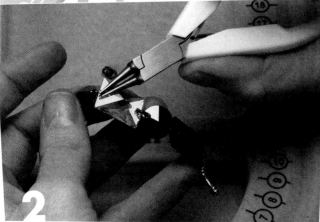

LINK SEW-ON STONES

LINK THE SEW-ON STONES TOGETHER WITH THE GUNMETAL JUMP RINGS IN THE PATTERN AS SHOWN.

FINISH NECKLACE

CONTINUE LINKING ALL OF THE SEW-ON STONES TOGETHER UNTIL YOU HAVE REACHED THE FINISHED LENGTH. ATTACH THE CIRCLE END OF THE TOGGLE TO THE FINAL SEW-ON STONE WITH A JUMP RING.

SUPERSTAR
BADGE + ID HOLDER

"YOU'RE A SUPERSTAR, THAT'S WHAT YOU ARE..." JUST BECAUSE YOU HAVE TO WORK IN A CUBICLE AND WEAR A DORKY BADGE DOESN'T MEAN YOU CAN'T BE THE QUEEN OF THE WATER COOLER!

This totally over-the-top crystal lanyard will make you feel like the superstar you truly are. Why be boring when you can be fabulous?

WHAT YOU WILL NEED

SUPPLIES
* 30" (76cm) Swarovski crystal square channel chain (buy the individual channels and hook them together with small jump rings if you can't find the premade chain)
* **8** 8mm Swarovski crystal cubes
* **8** 8mm Swarovski black diamond cubes
* **8** 8mm Swarovski black crystal pearls
* **7** 20mm Swarovski crystal stars
* large SP or sterling lobster clasp
* SP metal badge/lanyard holder
* **24** 22-gauge sterling head pins
* 10mm jump ring
* **7** 4mm jump rings

TOOLS
* snipe-nose pliers
* round-nose pliers
* oblique or flush cutters
* chain-nose pliers

94

RESOURCES: SWAROVSKI CRYSTAL CHAIN, PEARLS, CUBES AND STARS FROM SWAROVSKI; LANYARD SWIVEL, BADGE HOLDER AND JUMP RINGS FROM RINGS AND THINGS; STERLING FINDINGS FROM MARVIN SCHWAB

ATTACH LANYARD TO CHAIN

ATTACH THE LANYARD HOLDER TO ONE END OF THE SQUARE-CHANNEL CHAIN WITH A 10MM JUMP RING.

CREATE AND ATTACH DANGLES

CREATE EACH SQUARE CRYSTAL AND PEARL DANGLE BY SLIDING EACH BEAD ONTO A HEAD PIN AND CREATING A CLOSED LOOP AT THE TOP WITH ROUND-NOSE AND CHAIN-NOSE PLIERS (SEE TECHNIQUES, PAGE 16). PREPARE THE STARS BY SLIDING THEM ONTO 8MM JUMP RINGS. ATTACH THE DANGLES TO THE CHAIN EVERY TWO LINKS IN THE FOLLOWING PATTERN: BLACK CRYSTAL PEARL, CRYSTAL CUBE, BLACK DIAMOND CUBE, CRYSTAL STAR. ATTACH EACH DANGLE BY OPENING AND CLOSING THE HEAD PIN LOOPS WITH SNIPE-NOSE AND ROUND-NOSE PLIERS. ATTACH THE STARS TO THE CHAIN BY OPENING AND CLOSING THE JUMP RING AROUND THE PROPER LINK IN THE CHAIN.

FINISH BADGE HOLDER

ATTACH THE LOBSTER CLAW TO THE FINAL LINK IN THE CHAIN.

DESIGNER TIP

Sometimes less is more...and occasionally more is more! I couldn't help myself when I saw this Swarovski chain, I just wanted to keep on going to sparkly town...and so I did. Feel free to take it even further, as far as you can go and still walk through the office without feeling ridiculous!

quickie: DANCING QUEEN EARRINGS

Everyone knows that a Superstar really must have matching accessories. Put on your new Superstar Badge Holder and your Dancing Queen Earrings and you're likely to catch yourself belting out a tune. "You are the dancing queen, young and sweet, only seventeen." You'll be a superstar dancing queen!

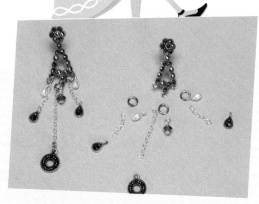

TO MAKE THESE SIMPLE SPARKLY EARRINGS, LINK THE CHARMS AND/OR BEADS OF YOUR CHOICE TO SHORT PIECES OF STERLING CHAIN. LINK THE TOP END OF EACH CHAIN TO THE CHANDELIER COMPONENT WITH A JUMP RING. AND YOU CAN ADD BEADS DIRECTLY TO THE CHANDELIER COMPONENT WITH JUMP RINGS AS WELL.

PREP SCHOOL PRINCESS
NECKLACE

PREMADE ROSARY CHAINS SPILL THROUGH A TOGGLE CLASP CIRCLE IN A WATER-FALL EFFECT IN THIS PIECE. The splashes of pink and mint green give this design a preppy feel. Add a matching grosgrain ribbon to your pony tail, a madras plaid shift and a woven wicker pocket book and head off to the clam bake with Biff Baxter.

WHAT YOU WILL NEED

SUPPLIES
* **6** 6mm pink cat's eye rounds
* **6** 6mm green cat's eye ovals
* approx. **12** 3mm green Swarovski crystal channels
* Magatama Toho clear AB seed beads
* Magatama Toho pink AB seed beads
* rosary chain
* 2½" (6cm) linked premade chain
* textured toggle clasp
* textured toggle clasp circle end
* approx. **15** silver head pins
* approx. **40** 4mm silver jump rings

TOOLS
* round-nose pliers
* snipe- or chain-nose pliers
* bead mat

RESOURCES: ROSARY CHAIN FROM JEWELRYSUPPLY.COM; JUMP RINGS AND BEADS FROM BEADALON; TOGGLE CLASPS WITH EXTENDERS FROM BLUE MOON BEADS

BUILD SHORT MULTISTRAND CHAIN

OPEN AND CLOSE LINKS ON THE PREMADE CHAIN WITH CHAIN-NOSE PLIERS TO CREATE THREE EQUAL STRANDS 6¾" (17CM) LONG. CONNECT EACH END OF EACH OF THE THREE STRANDS TO THE CIRCLE END OF A TOGGLE CLASP BY OPENING AND CLOSING THE WIRE ABOVE THE PEARL WITH THE CHAIN-NOSE PLIERS. CONNECT A 2½" (6CM) LINKED CHAIN TO ONE OF THE CIRCLES AS WELL.

MAKE MAGATAMA SEED BEAD DANGLES

CREATE THREE MORE LENGTHS OF ROSARY CHAIN, ONE 14½" (37CM), ONE 13" (33CM) AND ONE 10" (25CM). ATTACH ONE END OF EACH LENGTH OF CHAIN TO THE BAR END OF A TOGGLE CLASP. USE CHAIN-NOSE PLIERS TO OPEN A BASE METAL JUMP RING AND THREAD ON A SEED BEAD. REPEAT FOR ALL JUMP RINGS AND ATTACH THEM RANDOMLY TO THE FINAL 4" (10CM) OF THE ROSARY CHAIN.

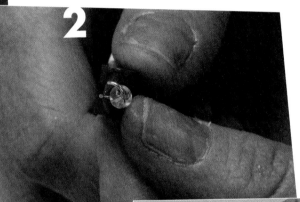

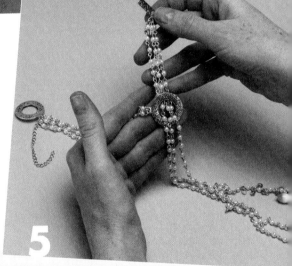

CREATE AND ATTACH CRYSTAL CHANNEL DANGLES

THREAD CRYSTAL CHANNELS ONTO JUMP RINGS AND THEN ADD THEM TO THE ROSARY CHAIN STRANDS.

ADD CAT'S EYE GLASS BEADS

THREAD THE CAT'S EYE GLASS BEADS ONTO HEAD PINS AND MAKE A LOOP AT THE TOP OF EACH ONE. THREAD ALL THREE BEADS ONTO ONE JUMP RING AND ATTACH THE JUMP RING TO THE BOTTOM OF THE LAST PEARL IN EACH STRAND OF CHAIN.

FINISH NECKLACE

YOU WILL NOW HAVE TWO SEPARATE PIECES. THE LONG STRANDS OF CHAIN HAVE ONE BAR TOGGLE CLASP ON ONE END AND BEADS AT THE OTHER END. THE SHORT CHAIN STRANDS ARE ATTACHED AT EITHER END TO THE CIRCLE PART OF A TOGGLE CLASP. TO FINISH THE NECKLACE, THREAD THE LONG PEARL STRANDS THROUGH ONE OF THE CIRCLE TOGGLE CLASPS OF THE SHORT MULTISTRAND OF PEARLS. SIMPLY THREAD THE TOGGLE THROUGH THE FREE CIRCLE TO SECURE THE NECKLACE AROUND YOUR NECK.

PATIENCE BOOSTER

Premade beaded rosary-style chain comes in a variety of styles and colors. Why make your own if you don't have to?

CRYSTAL COUTURE
NECKLACE

IN THIS NECKLACE, DRAPED LENGTHS OF MULTI-HUED CHANNEL CHAIN HANG FROM FILIGREE CRYSTAL FLOWERS LIKE THE ICING ON A SUPER-FANCY WEDDING CAKE.
Connecting the individual channels with small jump rings seems like it will take forever, but you will be surprised at how easy this necklace is to construct. Pretend it took forever and bask in the amazement of friends and family when you tell them you made it all by yourself.

WHAT YOU WILL NEED

SUPPLIES
* **20** 6mm x 4mm topaz two-ring open-back Swarovski channels
* **18** 6mm x 4mm indicolite two-ring open-back Swarovski channels
* **12** 6mm x 4mm Indian sapphire two-ring open-back Swarovski channels
* **7** 20mm indicolite and crystal filigree Swarovski flowers
* small SP toggle clasp
* **65** 4mm SP jump rings

TOOLS
* round-nose pliers
* short snipe- or chain-nose pliers
* bead board

RESOURCES: SWAROVSKI CRYSTAL CHANNELS AND FLOWERS FROM SWAROVSKI NORTH AMERICA; JUMP RINGS FROM RINGS AND THINGS; CLASP FROM BEADALON

MAKE "MAIN" CHAIN SEGMENTS

LINK THREE SWAROVSKI CHANNELS IN THE PATTERN AS
SHOWN IN THIS PICTURE (INDICOLITE, INDIAN SAPPHIRE,
TOPAZ) WITH 4MM SILVER JUMP RINGS USING SNIPE-NOSE
PLIERS. THIS LINKED CHAIN SEGMENT MAKES UP THE "MAIN"
OR "TOP" CHAIN OF THE NECKLACE.

MAKE "SWAG" CHAIN

LINK FIVE SWAROVSKI CHANNELS IN THE PATTERN AS SHOWN (TOPAZ,
INDICOLITE, INDIAN SAPPHIRE, TOPAZ, INDICOLITE) WITH 4MM SILVER
JUMP RINGS USING SNIPE-NOSE PLIERS. THIS LINKED CHAIN SEGMENT
MAKES UP THE "BOTTOM" OR "SWAG" CHAIN OF THE NECKLACE.

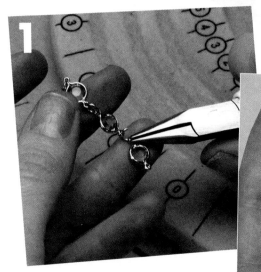

PATIENCE BOOSTER

If you just can't fathom connecting 65 jump rings, substitute premade chain for the channel links.
I think you will be surprised how
easy this is...think of it as a moving meditation!

ATTACH TOP AND SWAG CHANNEL
SEGMENTS TO CRYSTAL FLOWERS

ATTACH A THREE-CHANNEL SEGMENT TO A
CRYSTAL FLOWER PETAL ON EITHER SIDE
WITH 4MM JUMP RINGS. ATTACH ONE END
OF THE SWAG SEGMENT TO THE SAME
FLOWER PETAL BELOW THE FIRST JUMP
RING, AND THEN ATTACH THE OTHER END
OF THE SWAG SEGMENT TO THE OTHER
FLOWER PETAL. CONTINUE TO LINK THE
SWAG SEGMENTS TOGETHER UNTIL THE
DESIRED LENGTH IS REACHED.

ATTACH TOGGLE CLASP
TO CHAIN ENDS

ATTACH ONE TOPAZ CHANNEL
TO THE CIRCLE END OF THE TOG-
GLE CLASP AND ATTACH IT TO
THE FINAL BEADED SEGMENT ON
ONE END OF THE NECKLACE
WITH A JUMP RING. ATTACH THE
BAR SIDE OF THE TOGGLE CLASP
TO ANOTHER SINGLE TOPAZ
CHANNEL AND ATTACH IT TO
THE FINAL BEADED SEGMENT
WITH TWO LINKED JUMP RINGS.

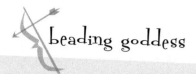

FAERIE QUEEN MAB'S
DRAGONFLY NECKLACE

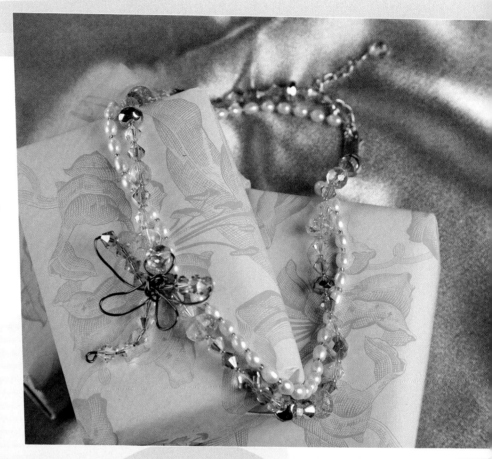

SEVERAL YEARS AGO, I HADN'T A PENNY WITH WHICH TO PURCHASE GIFTS FOR MY FRIENDS AND FAMILY.

I threw together wire and crystal bug ornaments, and they proved to be the doorway to a cool new career. This little dragonfly is a signature design for me, and once you get your bead groove on, you too will begin creating your own signature elements...I promise! Pearls, Swarovski crystal, vivid colors and a shimmering dragonfly combine in a necklace fit for the Faerie Queen Mab.

6MM X 8MM BRONZE FACETED CZECH GLASS DONUT

6MM JONQUIL SWAROVSKI BICONE

6MM LIGHT COLORADO TOPAZ SWAROVSKI BICONE

8MM CZECH GLASS GOLDEN YELLOW FACETED OVAL

8MM X 10MM TEAL CZECH GLASS CRACKLE DONUT

RESOURCES: CRYSTAL FROM SWAROVSKI CZECH GLASS FROM GREAT CRAFT WORKS; PEARLS FROM THUNDERBIRD SUPPLY; COLOURCRAFT WIRE, EXTENSION CHAIN, TOHO SEED BEADS AND WIRE FROM BEADALON; STERLING FINDINGS FROM MARVIN SCHWAB

WHAT YOU WILL NEED

SUPPLIES
* **60** 6mm freshwater pearls
* size 15 yellow Toho AB seed beads
* **30** 6mm light Colorado topaz Swarovski bicones
* **25** 6mm jonquil Swarovski bicones
* **8** 8mm Czech glass golden yellow faceted ovals
* **6** 6mm x 8mm bronze faceted Czech glass donuts
* **6** 8mm x 10mm teal Czech glass crackle donuts
* 2½" (6cm) medium curb chain
* large sterling lobster clasp
* 22-gauge head pin
* **4** no. 2 sterling crimp tubes
* **2** 8mm silver jump rings
* **2** 18" (46cm) lengths .013" (.33mm) 49 strand wire
* 20" (51cm) 20-gauge brown wire

TOOLS
* round-nose pliers
* short snipe- or chain-nose pliers
* oblique or flush cutters
* multichannel bead board
* safety glasses

MAKE DRAGONFLY HEAD

RUN YOUR HANDS DOWN A 20" (51CM) LENGTH OF BROWN WIRE, USING THE HEAT OF YOUR HANDS TO STRAIGHTEN AND SMOOTH IT. THREAD A YELLOW CZECH GLASS OVAL ONTO THE CENTER OF THE WIRE TO CREATE THE DRAGONFLY'S HEAD. FOLD THE WIRE, CRISS-CROSS IT, HOLD THE CROSSED WIRE BETWEEN YOUR THUMB AND FOREFINGER AND USE YOUR OTHER THUMB AND FOREFINGER TO TWIST THE WIRE AND SECURE THE BEAD. CONTINUOUSLY RUN YOUR HANDS DOWN THE WIRE TO KEEP IT STRAIGHT AND SMOOTH.

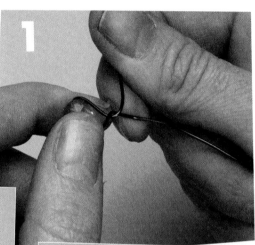

PATIENCE BOOSTER

Working with wire and glass takes practice, so I recommend that you practice before you attempt to create this necklace. This is one of those preparation saving-your-sanity thingies.

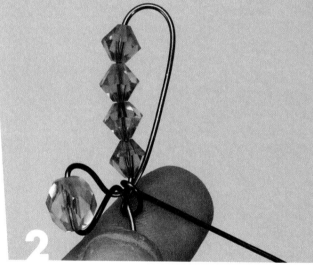

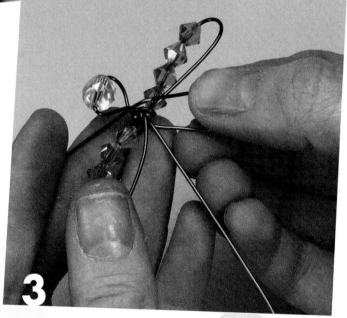

MAKE DRAGONFLY WINGS

SLIDE FOUR COLORADO TOPAZ BICONE BEADS ONTO ONE STRAND OF THE WIRE TO CREATE THE FIRST TOP WING OF THE DRAGONFLY. BEND THE WIRE INTO A WING SHAPE WITH YOUR FINGERS. CROSS THE WIRE TO THE LEFT OF THE "HEAD" AND THEN WRAP IT OVER THE OTHER END OF THE WIRE AND BEND IT UNDER THAT SAME WIRE, MAKING A LOOP. THEN BEND THE WIRE UP AND OVER THE RIGHT SIDE WING WIRES AND UNDER BOTH WIRES TO SECURE THE WING. KEEP SMOOTHING THE WIRE WITH YOUR HANDS AS YOU WORK. REPEAT ON THE OTHER SIDE TO CREATE THE LEFT WING, WORKING OVER, UNDER, OVER AND UNDER TO THE LEFT SIDE.

MAKE LOWER WINGS

LOOP THE WIRE INTO A LOWER WING ON THE RIGHT SIDE AND REPEAT ON THE LEFT SIDE, WRAPPING THE WIRE SECURELY AROUND THE CROSSED WIRES UNDER THE DRAGONFLY'S HEAD.

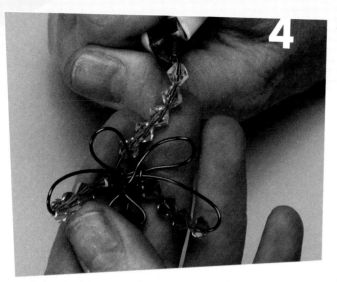

MAKE DRAGONFLY TAIL

THREAD FIVE JONQUIL BICONE BEADS ONTO ONE WIRE TO CREATE THE DRAGONFLY'S TAIL. USE FLUSH CUTTERS TO TRIM THE WIRE TO ABOUT ³⁄₁₆" (5MM) ABOVE THE BEAD AND CREATE A SMALL LOOP WITH THE ROUND-NOSE PLIERS TO SECURE THE BEADS. MANIPULATE THE TAIL AND THE WINGS AS YOU WISH.

DESIGNER TIP

Wear safety goggles when you are working with wire and glass. Tiny little shards of glass can break off and fly through the air. Believe me, trying to get a tiny glass shard out of your eye to avoid a trip to the emergency room is really, really stressful.

STRING NECKLACE AND ATTACH DRAGONFLY

ATTACH AN 18" (46CM) LENGTH OF WIRE TO THE LOBSTER CLASP. THREAD PEARLS AND SEED BEADS ONTO THIS STRAND, ALTERNATING BETWEEN THEM. AT THE 30TH BEAD, LEAVE OUT THE SEED BEAD BETWEEN THE PEARLS. CONTINUE BEADING TO THE END OF THE STRAND. CONNECT ANOTHER PIECE OF WIRE TO THE LOBSTER CLASP. STRING THE SECOND STRAND OF BEADS IN THE PATTERN AS SHOWN ON PAGE 100, STARTING WITH TWO TOPAZ BICONE CRYSTALS: JONQUIL BICONE, BRONZE CZECH GLASS DONUT, JONQUIL BICONE, TOPAZ BICONE, CZECH GLASS YELLOW OVAL, TOPAZ BICONE. STRING ON A SEED BEAD AFTER EACH CRYSTAL. STRING ON AN ADDITIONAL TOPAZ BICONE TO FINISH THE STRAND. ATTACH EACH WIRE TO A JUMP RING. ATTACH THE DRAGONFLY TO THE CENTER OF THE TWO STRANDS, MARKED BY THE SPOT WHERE THERE IS NO SEED BEAD BETWEEN THE PEARLS. ATTACH IT BY WRAPPING THE REMAINDER OF THE SECOND WIRE AROUND THE MIDDLE OF THE BEADED STRANDS AND THEN WRAP THE EXCESS WIRE AROUND THE BASE OF THE LOOP (LIKE A LOOSE WRAPPED LOOP).

FINISH NECKLACE

ATTACH A 2½" (6CM) LENGTH OF MEDIUM CURB CHAIN TO THE JUMP RING AT THE END OF THE NECKLACE. SLIDE A COLORADO TOPAZ BEAD ONTO A HEAD PIN AND MAKE A SMALL LOOP AT THE TOP. CONNECT THE BEAD TO THE LAST LINK IN THE CHAIN.

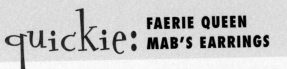

quickie: FAERIE QUEEN MAB'S EARRINGS

It's a snap to whip up these dazzling earrings to match your new creation. Use the beads I selected here, or create your own unique combination.

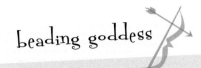
PROM QUEEN
CHOKER

THIS VICTORIAN-INSPIRED NECKLACE LOOKS LIKE YOU FOUND IT IN AN ANTIQUE STORE.

The gunmetal findings give it a vintage feel and the muted color palette adds a touch of under-stated elegance. This sparkly number would look fabulous with a Victorian-style lace and linen blouse and distressed jeans...or pull out all the stops and wear it with a simple evening gown. You may not have been the prom queen in high school, but you can feel like one when you wear this design.

BEADED SEGMENT A

4MM BLACK DIAMOND AB SWAROVSKI BICONE

6MM CRYSTAL AB DONUT

BEADED SEGMENT B

4MM LIGHT PEACH SWAROVSKI BICONE

WHAT YOU WILL NEED

SUPPLIES

* ✳ **18** 3mm light azore Swarovski rounds
* ✳ **32** 4mm light peach Swarovski bicones
* ✳ **12** 3mm crystal vitrial medium Swarovski rounds
* ✳ **29** 6mm crystal AB donuts
* ✳ **30** 4mm black diamond AB Swarovski bicones
* ✳ **6** 9mm x 6mm black diamond teardrops
* ✳ **6** 9mm x 6mm crystal teardrops
* ✳ **27** gunmetal head pins
* ✳ approx. **45** gunmetal eye pins
* ✳ **57** 4mm gunmetal jump rings

TOOLS

* ✳ round-nose pliers
* ✳ short snipe- or chain-nose pliers
* ✳ oblique or flush cutters
* ✳ bead board

RESOURCES: CRYSTAL FROM SWAROVSKI; GUNMETAL FINDINGS FROM RINGS AND THINGS; TOOLS FROM LINDSTROM TOOLS

BEGIN TO MAKE CLASP

BEND AN EYE PIN INTO A "U" SHAPE WITH YOUR FINGERS. MAKE A SMALL LOOP AT THE VERY END OF THE EYE PIN WITH THE ROUND-NOSE PLIERS.

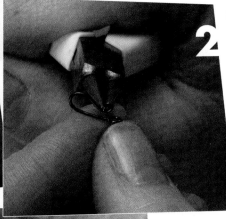

FINISH CLASP

USE THE SHORT SNIPE-NOSE PLIERS TO BEND THE LOOP YOU JUST MADE SO THAT IT IS PERPENDICULAR TO THE EYE PIN LOOP.

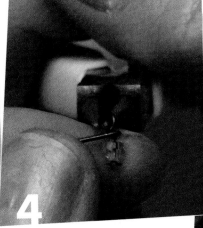

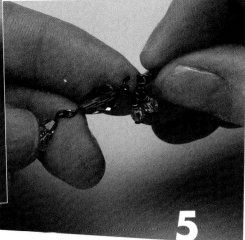

CREATE BEADED SEGMENTS

CREATE THE BEADED SEGMENTS THAT MAKE UP THE CORE CHAIN AS SHOWN IN THE DIAGRAM ON PAGE 103. ATTACH BEADED SEGMENT **A** TO THE CLASP YOU MADE WITH A JUMP RING. USE A JUMP RING TO LINK BEADED SEGMENT **B** TO THE FIRST BEADED SEGMENT AND CONTINUE TO LINK SEGMENTS A AND B TOGETHER (ALTERNATING BETWEEN THE TWO) UNTIL YOU REACH THE FINISHED LENGTH.

CREATE SMALL DANGLES

CREATE THE SMALLEST COMPONENT OF THE DANGLES BY SLIDING A 3MM VITRIAL ROUND ONTO A HEAD PIN AND CREATE A WRAPPED LOOP BY TWISTING THE WIRE WITH THE VERY TIP OF THE CHAIN-NOSE PLIERS. MAKE 18 LIGHT AZORE AND 12 CRYSTAL VITRIAL DROPS.

FINISH WATERFALL DANGLES

CREATE THE MAIN DANGLES BY LINKING BEADED SEGMENTS IN THE PATTERNS AS SHOWN IN STEP SIX. ATTACH THREE TINY DANGLES ONTO THE VERY END OF EACH LARGE DANGLE BY INSERTING THEM ONTO A JUMP RING.

FINISH DANGLES

CREATE ALL OF THE REMAINING DANGLES AND LAY THEM OUT ON YOUR WORK SURFACE. CREATE A TOTAL OF NINE DANGLES: TWO OF DANGLE **1**, FOUR OF DANGLE **2**, TWO OF DANGLE **3**, AND ONE OF DANGLE **4**. THE DANGLES ARE BEADED AS FOLLOWS (FROM LEFT TO RIGHT):

DANGLE #1: PEACH BICONE, CRYSTAL AB DONUT, PEACH BICONE, BLACK DIAMOND TEARDROP WITH THREE AZORE DANGLES

DANGLE #2: CRYSTAL TEARDROP WITH THREE LIGHT VITRIAL DANGLES

DANGLE #3: BLACK DIAMOND BICONE, CRYSTAL AB DONUT, BLACK DIAMOND BICONE, PEACH BICONE, CRYSTAL AB DONUT, PEACH BICONE, BLACK DIAMOND TEARDROP WITH THREE AZORE DANGLES

DANGLE #4: PEACH BICONE, CRYSTAL AB DONUT, PEACH BICONE, BLACK DIAMOND BICONE, CRYSTAL AB DONUT, BLACK DIAMOND BICONE, PEACH BICONE, CRYSTAL AB DONUT, PEACH PICONE, BLACK DIAMOND TEARDROP WITH THREE AZORE DANGLES

MAKE DECORATIVE CHAIN

LINK 16 GUNMETAL JUMP RINGS TOGETHER, AND ATTACH THEM TO THE LAST BEADED SEGMENT OF THE CHAIN.

ATTACH DANGLES TO CHAIN

ATTACH THE DANGLES TO THE CHAIN YOU CREATED BY OPENING AND CLOSING A JUMP RING, LINKING THE FIRST DANGLE TO THE EIGHTH JUMP RING FROM THE CLASP. ATTACH A DANGLE TO EACH SUBSEQUENT JUMP RING IN THE FOLLOWING ORDER: DANGLE **1**, DANGLE **2**, DANGLE **3**, DANGLE **2**, DANGLE **4**, DANGLE **2**, DANGLE **3**, DANGLE **2**, DANGLE **1**.

PATIENCE BOOSTER

This one takes time and a bit of patience...it is easy to lose your place in the design. I highly recommend you give yourself a few hours to complete this and work without too many distractions. Just think of the sense of accomplishment you'll feel when you finish!

MAKE DECORATIVE DANGLE

CONSTRUCT A DANGLE BY LINKING THREE TINY CRYSTAL DANGLES ON A JUMP RING TO A BLACK DIAMOND TEARDROP-SHAPED CRYSTAL. CONNECT THE DANGLE TO THE END OF THE CHAIN YOU CONSTRUCTED.

quickie:

PROM QUEEN EARRINGS

With these sparkly earrings and your matching choker, you'll be the belle of the ball. You're bound to have a few extra crystals left over when you finish the necklace. Put them to good use by threading them on head and eye pins, connecting them into dangles and attaching them to the earring form with jump rings.

USE A PREMADE CHANDELIER EARRING COMPONENT TO MAKE MATCHING EARRINGS. SIMPLY LINK SEVERAL BEADED DANGLES TO THE METAL CIRCLES ON THE EARRING FORM.

over the edge

CONGRATULATIONS...YOU HAVE OFFICIALLY CROSSED OVER TO THE OTHER SIDE! THINK OF THE PROJECTS IN THIS SECTION AS BEAD TEASERS, DIFFICULT DESIGNS TO TEST YOUR NEWLY FOUND PATIENCE AND YOUR BLOSSOMING BEAD SKILLS. YOU HAVE BEEN DULY WARNED OF THE PERILS THAT MIGHT LIE AHEAD—NOW GO FORTH AND CREATE.

This is the fun part...really! You have mastered the basics, and now you can begin to define and develop your own personal style. As you begin to experiment, take my designs and adjust them to fit your tastes. Maybe you'd like to try a piece in your own favorite color combination. Maybe you'd like to add an additional strand or two to this or that piece. Maybe one of the pieces in this section will spark an idea for a completely new design, created entirely by you. Work without a net, defy the laws of physics and forge new pathways into the world of jewelry design. These designs are all about stretching yourself in new directions. And don't worry about all the little (or big) "mess-ups" you might encounter along the way. Just cut the string or wire and start again, because you won't arrive at your perfect necklace or bracelet via the easy route. Take the long and bumpy way around, and you might just learn a few things. All hail the Bead Queen!

"THINK LIKE A QUEEN. A QUEEN IS NOT AFRAID TO FAIL. FAILURE IS ANOTHER STEPPING STONE TO GREATNESS."
—OPRAH WINFREY

TECHNIQUES

- MULTISTRAND BEADED EMBELLISHMENTS
- WEAVING EXPOSED WIRE
- SO MANY HEAD PINS, SO LITTLE TIME
- EXPOSED MULTI-WIRE STATIONS
- PULLING OUT ALL THE STOPS

EARTH MOTHER
AUTUMN LEAVES NECKLACE

REMEMBER THE PAPER CHAINS YOU MADE IN GRADE SCHOOL?
This necklace is a grown-up version with autumnal shaded seed beads and semiprecious gemstones. This one is easy once you master the technique, but it still looks really impressive to those who don't know the trick! Become a bead magician, and you won't have to divulge your secrets—it's the first rule of magic, don't you know?

10MM PUFFY JADE SQUARE BEAD

SIZE 11 FOREST GREEN SEED BEAD

SIZE 11 RUST SEED BEAD

SIZE 11 GOLDEN YELLOW SEED BEAD

SIZE 11 BROWN SEED BEAD

15MM CARNELIAN DONUT DISC BEAD

WHAT YOU WILL NEED

SUPPLIES
* **13** 10mm puffy jade square beads
* **12** 15mm carnelian donut disc beads
* **1** tube size 11 forest green seed beads
* **1** tube size 11 rust seed beads
* **1** tube size 11 golden yellow seed beads
* **1** tube size 11 brown seed beads
* sterling silver toggle clasp
* **2** no. 2 sterling crimp tubes
* 40" (102cm) .013" (.33mm) 19 or 49 strand wire

TOOLS
* crimp tool
* oblique or flush cutters
* bead mat

RESOURCES: GEMSTONE BEADS FROM PHOENIX BEADS, JEWELRY AND PARTS; SEED BEADS FROM BLUE MOON BEADS; STERLING FINDINGS FROM MARVIN SCHWAB; WIRE FROM BEADALON

BEGIN BEADING NECKLACE

ATTACH THE CIRCLE END OF THE TOGGLE CLASP TO ONE DOUBLED 40"
(102CM) LENGTH OF WIRE WITH A CRIMP TUBE. THREAD ONE PUFFY
JADE SQUARE BEAD ONTO BOTH STRANDS OF WIRE. SEPARATE THE
WIRES AND FEED TWO FOREST GREEN SEED BEADS, TWO RUST, TWO
GOLDEN YELLOW AND TWO BROWN SEED BEADS ONTO EACH
STRAND, AS SHOWN IN THE DIAGRAM.

WEAVE ON DISK BEAD

FEED ONE WIRE THROUGH THE HOLE IN THE CARNELIAN DISK AND
THEN FEED ONE BROWN SEED BEAD ONTO ONE OF THE WIRES. FEED
THE OTHER WIRE THROUGH THE SAME BROWN SEED BEAD IN THE
OPPOSITE DIRECTION SO THE TWO WIRES CRISSCROSS INSIDE THE
SEED BEAD. PULL THE WIRES TAUT.

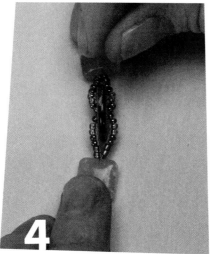

CONTINUE TO STRING BEADS

THREAD TWO BROWN, TWO GOLDEN
YELLOW, TWO RUST AND TWO FOREST
GREEN SEED BEADS ONTO EACH WIRE.
FEED BOTH WIRES THROUGH A SQUARE
JADE BEAD.

CHECK BEADING PROGRESS FROM SIDE

AFTER STRINGING ON THE FIRST PATTERN SEGMENT,
TURN THE PIECE TO THE SIDE TO MAKE SURE YOU
HAVE WOVEN THE DISC INTO THE NECKLACE
PROPERLY. THIS IS HOW IT SHOULD LOOK!

FINISH NECKLACE

CONTINUE BEADING THE NECKLACE IN THE
ESTABLISHED PATTERN UNTIL YOU REACH THE
FINAL BEAD. SLIDE BOTH WIRE STRANDS
THROUGH A CRIMP TUBE, THROUGH THE BAR
END OF THE TOGGLE CLASP AND BACK
THROUGH THE CRIMP TUBE. FLATTEN WITH THE
CRIMP TOOL (SEE TECHNIQUES, PAGE 14).

DESIGNER TIP

I love the earthy look this color palette
provides, but you can create an entirely different palette using different graduated colors of seed beads and core
beads. I know I keep harping on this,
but once you find your inner designer
and set her free, you will be so glad
that you did!

PARVATI'S HINDU JEWELS
BRACELET

IN THIS WOVEN BRACELET FIT FOR A HINDU GODDESS, BEAUTIFUL RICH SHADES OF PURPLE, TEAL AND RASPBERRY PINK COMBINE IN A ROMANTIC, DIMENSIONAL AND TEXTURED DESIGN.

The clasp is made from a Swarovski crystal button and seed-beaded loop which give this bracelet a real designer appeal. By changing the color palette and bead shapes, you will get an entirely different look with the same techniques—try it! Throw this bracelet on with a gauzy peasant blouse to rock the Boho hippie girl look.

WHAT YOU WILL NEED

SUPPLIES

* **6** 12mm purple dyed faceted pillow-cut square quartz beads
* **6** 4mm x 6mm lavender Czech glass donuts
* **6** 3mm x 5mm raspberry Czech glass donuts
* **6** 3mm x 5mm teal Czech glass donuts
* **1** tube size 11 light blue seed beads
* **1** tube size 11 deep blue seed beads
* sage Swarovski crystal button
* **2** no. 2 silver crimp tubes
* 24" (61cm) .015" (.38mm) 19 or 49 strand wire

TOOLS

* crimp tool
* oblique or flush cutters
* bead mat

RESOURCES: CZECH GLASS BEADS FROM YORK NOVELTY; QUARTZ FROM PHOENIX JEWELRY AND PARTS; SEED BEADS FROM BLUE MOON BEADS; CRIMP TUBES AND SWAROVSKI BUTTON FROM JEWELRYSUPPLY.COM; WIRE FROM BEADALON

CREATE BEADED LOOP

DOUBLE A 24" (61CM) LENGTH OF WIRE.
STRING ON 24 DEEP BLUE SEED BEADS
AND SLIDE THEM TO THE BEND IN THE
WIRE. SLIDE A STERLING SILVER CRIMP TUBE
ONTO BOTH STRANDS AND PULL IT SNUG
AGAINST THE SEED BEADS TO CREATE A
LOOP. USE THE CRIMP TOOL TO FLATTEN
THE CRIMP TUBE AND FOLD IT OVER.

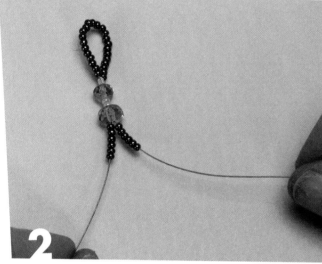

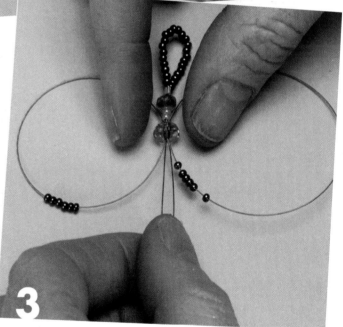

STRING ON FIRST BEADED SEGMENT

THREAD A RASPBERRY DONUT BEAD AND TWO LIGHT
BLUE SEED BEADS ONTO BOTH STRANDS OF WIRE.
FEED BOTH WIRES THROUGH A LAVENDER DONUT
BEAD. NOW SEPARATE THE WIRES AND THREAD SIX
DEEP BLUE SEED BEADS ONTO EACH WIRE.

CREATE SEED BEAD LOOPS

THREAD EACH OF THE TWO WIRES BACK THROUGH THE LAVENDER
DONUT BEAD BY LOOPING EACH WIRE OUT TO THE SIDE AND UP AND
BACK DOWN THROUGH THE CENTER OF THE LAVENDER DONUT. MAKE
SURE TO USE YOUR FINGERS TO KEEP THE LAVENDER DONUT FLUSH
AGAINST THE LIGHT BLUE SEED BEADS. PULL THE STRANDS TIGHT. MAKE
SURE NOT TO CRISSCROSS THE WIRES INSIDE THE LAVENDER BEAD.

PATIENCE BOOSTER

Take the time to work the wire through the beads as you progress; check back and tighten the design before you finish. The tension has to be just right—not too tight and not too loose—for the design to fall properly when finished. Far better to get it right before you crimp so you don't have to start all over!

FINISH BRACELET

REPEAT THE PATTERN UNTIL YOU HAVE USED ALL OF THE BEADS, ENDING WITH A SQUARE PURPLE QUARTZ BEAD. FEED BOTH WIRES THROUGH A CRIMP TUBE AND THEN THROUGH THE BUTTON AND BACK THROUGH THE CRIMP TUBE. USE YOUR CRIMP TOOL TO FLATTEN THE CRIMP TUBE AND CUT OFF THE EXCESS WIRE WITH OBLIQUE CUTTERS.

CONTINUE STRINGING BEADS

THREAD TWO LIGHT BLUE SEED BEADS ONTO BOTH WIRES. SLIDE A RASPBERRY DONUT BEAD AND A FACETED SQUARE PURPLE QUARTZ BEAD ONTO BOTH STRANDS OF WIRE. SLIDE ON A TEAL DONUT BEAD AND THEN TWO DEEP BLUE SEED BEADS. FEED BOTH STRANDS THROUGH A LAVENDER DONUT BEAD. THEN SEPARATE THE TWO STRANDS AND FEED SIX LIGHT BLUE SEED BEADS ONTO EACH WIRE AND REPEAT THE BUTTERFLY LOOPING TECHNIQUE. PULL THE STRANDS TIGHT TO CREATE SEED BEAD LOOPS AROUND THE LAVENDER DONUT BEAD.

MERMAID'S BOUNTY
NECKLACE

I ENVISIONED PEARLS SUSPENDED ON WIRE, IN AN ORGANIC AND UNSTRUCTURED WAY, WHEN I CREATED THIS PIECE. I love the movement the beaded stations create and the random look this technique reflects. This is one of my attempts to defy physics, and I am still working on making a multiple-wire stationed DNA strand design...even the impatient can be obsessive-compulsive when inspiration strikes!

WHAT YOU WILL NEED

SUPPLIES
* **40** 8mm black Swarovski crystal pearls
* **40** 8mm powder almond Swarovski crystal pearls
* **40** 8mm bright gold Swarovski crystal pearls
* **40** 8mm brown Swarovski crystal pearls
* extra large sterling silver lobster clasp
* **3** 6mm sterling silver oval jump rings
* **4** no. 4 crimp tubes
* **4** 20" (51cm) strands .018" (.46mm) 19 or 49 strand silver-plated wire

TOOLS
* mighty crimp tool
* short snipe-nose pliers or chain-nose pliers
* oblique or flush cutters
* bead mat

RESOURCES: CRYSTAL PEARLS FROM SWAROVSKI; CRIMPS AND SILVER-PLATED WIRE FROM BEADALON

DOUBLE CRIMP WIRES

THREAD ALL FOUR WIRES THROUGH A NO. 4 CRIMP TUBE, LEAVING 2" (5CM) OF WIRE FREE. FLATTEN THE CRIMP TUBE WITH THE MIGHTY CRIMP TOOL. THREAD ALL OF THE WIRES THROUGH ANOTHER NO. 4 CRIMP TUBE, THROUGH THE LOBSTER CLASP AND BACK THROUGH THE CRIMP TUBE—YOU MAY NEED TO USE CHAIN-NOSE PLIERS TO PULL THE EIGHT-WIRE THICKNESS THROUGH THE CRIMP TUBES, AS IT IS A TIGHT FIT.

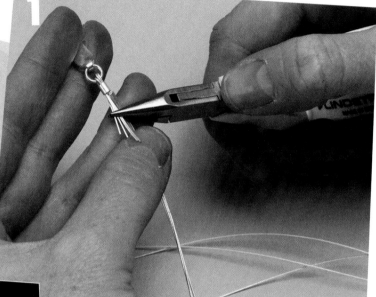

DESIGNER TIP

If you use randomly shaped beads here, you will get an entirely different finished effect. Try colored wires and brightly colored beads for a fun and funky party necklace. The mighty crimp tool and large crimp tubes open up a whole new world of design possibilities.

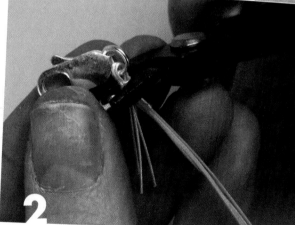

FOLD CRIMP TUBE

FLATTEN THE CRIMP TUBE WITH THE MIGHTY CRIMP TOOL AND FOLD IT IN HALF TO SECURE IT. CUT OFF THE WIRE TAILS WITH FLUSH CUTTERS.

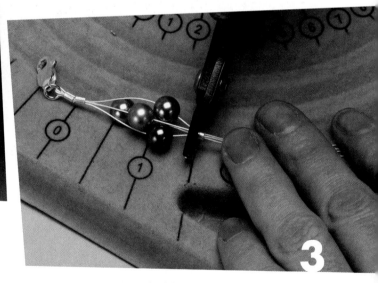

SECURE FIRST PEARL CLUSTER

SEPARATE THE STRANDS AND STRING ONE PEARL OF A DIFFERENT COLOR ONTO EACH STRAND. THREAD ALL FOUR STRANDS THROUGH A CRIMP TUBE, MEASURING 1 ½" (4CM) FROM THE END OF THE FIRST CRIMP TUBE TO THE END OF THE SECOND CRIMP TUBE. FLATTEN THE CRIMP TUBE WITH THE MIGHTY CRIMP TOOL AND FOLD IT IN HALF.

CONTINUE SECURING PEARL CLUSTERS

THREAD ON THE NEXT CLUSTER OF PEARLS AND SECURE IT
AS IN STEP THREE WITH ANOTHER CRIMP TUBE.

DESIGNER TIP

You can take the time to thread the
pearl wires so that they are not twisted
within each other, or allow them to
randomly and organically arrange
themselves as they will. It's all up to
your own aesthetic sense.

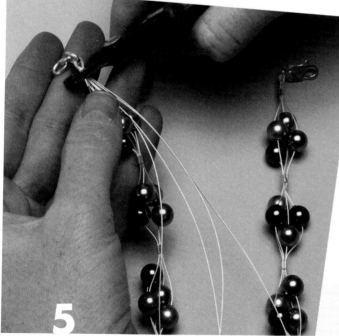

DOUBLE CRIMP END OF NECKLACE

DOUBLE CRIMP THE END OF THE NECKLACE, JUST AS AT
THE BEGINNING, USING TWO NO. 4 CRIMP TUBES.
ATTACH THREE STERLING SILVER JUMP RINGS ONTO THE
CLASP TO ADD A LITTLE MORE LENGTH, IF NECESSARY.

TRIM WIRE TAILS

CUT THE EXCESS WIRE WITH FLUSH CUTTERS, CUTTING IT EXACTLY FLUSH
AGAINST THE CRIMP TUBE. TRIMMING THE WIRE FLUSH TO THE CRIMP
TUBES PREVENTS THE WIRES FROM SCRATCHING THE WEARER.

WHIRLING DERVISH
BRACELET

THIS BRACELET USES SILVER-PLATED WIRE AS A DESIGN ELEMENT TO CREATE AN OPEN, WOVEN LOOK.

The key to success here is keeping the loops the same size. This one is far easier than it looks and really is pretty on the wrist. For some reason, it reminds me of a fancier, sparklier version of something you might have made at summer camp. Dress up your Bermuda shorts and tank tops with this woven wonder.

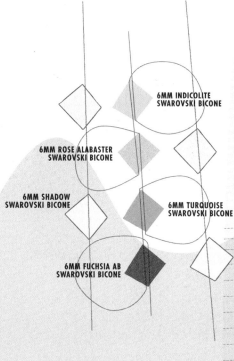

6MM INDICOLITE
SWAROVSKI BICONE

6MM ROSE ALABASTER
SWAROVSKI BICONE

6MM SHADOW
SWAROVSKI BICONE

6MM TURQUOISE
SWAROVSKI BICONE

6MM FUCHSIA AB
SWAROVSKI BICONE

RESOURCES: CRYSTAL FROM SWAROVSKI; STERLING FINDINGS FROM MARVIN SCHWAB; SILVER-PLATED WIRE FROM BEADALON

WHAT YOU WILL NEED

SUPPLIES

* **24** 6mm turquoise Swarovski bicones
* **24** 6mm rose alabaster Swarovski bicones
* **24** 6mm indicolite Swarovski bicones
* **24** 6mm fuchsia AB Swarovski bicones
* **24** 6mm shadow crystal Swarovski bicones
* large sterling lobster clasp
* **8** no. 3 sterling silver crimp tubes
* **2** 4mm oval sterling jump rings
* **2** 7" (18cm) lengths and 1 15" (38cm) length .015" (.38mm) 49 strand silver-plated wire

TOOLS

* crimp tool
* oblique or flush cutters
* bead mat

LOOP WIRE AROUND FIRST CRYSTAL

ATTACH THREE STRANDS OF SILVER-COATED WIRE INDIVIDUALLY TO A 4MM OVAL JUMP RING WITH CRIMP TUBES (LONGEST STRAND IN THE MIDDLE). STRING AN INDICOLITE BLUE 6MM BICONE CRYSTAL ONTO THE CENTER WIRE, AND BRING THE WIRE UP AND TO THE RIGHT AND BACK THROUGH THE SAME BEAD, CREATING A LOOP ON ONE SIDE OF THE BEAD.

LOOP ON NEXT BEAD

STRING THE NEXT BEAD IN THE PATTERN, A ROSE ALABASTER BICONE, ONTO THE CENTER WIRE. BRING THE WIRE UP AND TO THE OPPOSITE SIDE FROM THE LAST BEAD AND BACK THROUGH THE ROSE BEAD. YOU MUST BE CAREFUL TO MAKE SURE THAT THE LOOPS HAVE EVEN TENSION AND ARE THE SAME SIZE. DON'T WORRY AT THIS POINT, HOWEVER, IF THINGS DON'T LOOK EXACTLY RIGHT. CONTINUE STRINGING CRYSTALS AND LOOPING THE WIRE IN THE FOLLOWING PATTERN UNTIL YOU REACH THE DESIRED LENGTH: INDICOLITE BLUE, ROSE ALABASTER, TURQUOISE, FUCHSIA.

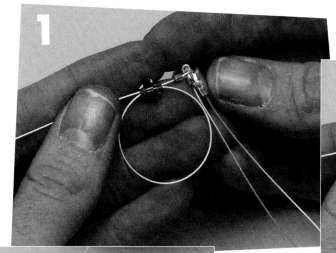

STRING SHADOW CRYSTALS ON OUTSIDE WIRES

STRING A SHADOW CRYSTAL ONTO AN OUTSIDE STRAND. WEAVE THE WIRE STRAND THROUGH THE FIRST LOOP.

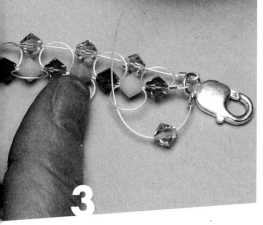

WEAVE WIRE THROUGH LOOPS

PULL THE WIRE STRAND TO THE RIGHT TENSION, STRING ON A SHADOW CRYSTAL AND CONTINUE TO WEAVE THE WIRE UNDER AND OVER, THROUGH EACH LOOP, CONTINUING TO PULL THE WIRE UNTIL YOU ACHIEVE THE CORRECT TENSION. THREAD ON A SHADOW CRYSTAL AFTER EACH LOOP. REPEAT FOR THE REMAINING OUTSIDE STRAND.

ATTACH CLASP

ADD THE CLASP AT THE END BY ATTACHING EACH OF THE WIRES TO A JUMP RING WITH A CRIMP TUBE. TRIM AWAY THE WIRE TAILS WITH FLUSH CUTTERS.

PATIENCE BOOSTER

Try this with a different color palette, but know that if you change the bead style or size, you will probably need to change your wire diameter to accommodate the different size holes of your beads. Remember to create the proper tension for the bracelet to maintain its shape.

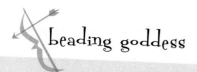

PROUD PEACOCK
NECKLACE

HAVE YOU EVER SEEN A PEACOCK STRUT HIS STUFF?

Man, is it impressive! My wonderful editor and I took a research trip to the Cincinnati Zoo and saw a peacock, who, jealous of all of the attention the pink flamingoes were getting, jumped into their habitat and went to town. This design was inspired by the colors, shape and iridescence of a peacock feather which I recreated using earthy dyed pearls and dyed abalone shell beads.

5MM BRONZE COIN PEARL

5MM X 7MM BLACK ONYX BAMBOO BEAD

15MM X 20MM DYED ORANGE ABALONE OVAL DOUBLET

5MM FIRE COIN PEARL

WHAT YOU WILL NEED

SUPPLIES
* **15** 15mm x 20mm dyed orange abalone oval doublets
* **49** 5mm bronze coin pearls
* **49** 5mm fire coin pearls
* **14** 5mm x 7mm small black onyx bamboo beads
* sterling hook and eye clasp
* **2** no. 2 sterling crimp tubes
* 40" (102cm) .013" (.33mm) 49 strand wire

TOOLS
* oblique or flush cutters
* crimp tool
* bead mat

RESOURCES: PEARLS AND BAMBOO BEADS FROM THUNDERBIRD SUPPLY; ABALONE DOUBLETS FROM GREAT CRAFT WORKS; STERLING FINDINGS FROM MARVIN SCHWAB; WIRE FROM BEADALON

STRING ON FIRST BEADED SEGMENT

ATTACH A 40" (102CM) STRAND OF WIRE TO A CLASP USING A CRIMP TUBE. STRING ON ONE ORANGE ABALONE SHELL. THEN BEGIN STRINGING ON THE BRONZE COIN PEARLS.

CREATE BRONZE PEARL ARC

STRING ON SEVEN BRONZE PEARLS, WITH THE FLAT SIDE FACING THE BACK, AND THREAD THE WIRE UP AND TO THE LEFT AND BACK THROUGH THE ORANGE ABALONE SHELL, CREATING AN ARC WITH THE BRONZE PEARLS.

PATIENCE BOOSTER

If you want the top-drilled pearls to fall identically within the design, I suggest you lay them out before you begin stringing. I gave the design a funky and organic look by randomly threading the pearls...but I am kooky like that!

CREATE RED PEARL ARC

STRING ON A BLACK ONYX BEAD AND THEN STRING ON ANOTHER ORANGE ABALONE BEAD. THREAD ON SEVEN FIRE COIN PEARLS. THREAD THE WIRE UP AND TO THE LEFT AND BACK THROUGH THE ORANGE ABALONE BEAD, AND THREAD ON ANOTHER BLACK ONYX BEAD AS BEFORE.

FINISH NECKLACE

CONTINUE STRINGING THE BEADS IN THE ESTABLISHED PATTERN UNTIL YOU REACH THE FINAL SEGMENT. FINISH THE NECKLACE BY ATTACHING THE OTHER END OF THE HOOK AND EYE CLASP, AFTER ADJUSTING THE WIRES TO ESTABLISH THE CORRECT TENSION.

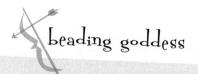
CHA-CHA-CHA
BRACELET

THIS IS THE MOST TIME-CONSUMING PROJECT IN THE BOOK, BE FOREWARNED.
I'm serious, this lovely little number takes hours. If you aren't prepared to deal with creating and attaching 168 beaded head pins, I suggest that you move on to the next project. Are you still here? Good for you! You can't get much more sparkle and movement than this over-the-top cha-cha bracelet offers. Throw on an off-the-shoulder top, strappy ball room dance sandals and a flirty skirt and cha cha cha!

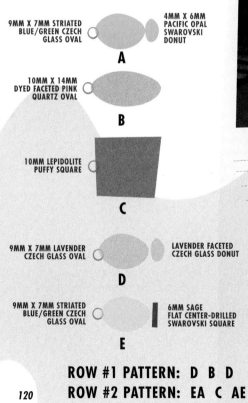

9MM X 7MM STRIATED BLUE/GREEN CZECH GLASS OVAL — 4MM X 6MM PACIFIC OPAL SWAROVSKI DONUT

A

10MM X 14MM DYED FACETED PINK QUARTZ OVAL

B

10MM LEPIDOLITE PUFFY SQUARE

C

9MM X 7MM LAVENDER CZECH GLASS OVAL — LAVENDER FACETED CZECH GLASS DONUT

D

9MM X 7MM STRIATED BLUE/GREEN CZECH GLASS OVAL — 6MM SAGE FLAT CENTER-DRILLED SWAROVSKI SQUARE

E

ROW #1 PATTERN: D B D
ROW #2 PATTERN: EA C AE

WHAT YOU WILL NEED

SUPPLIES
* **21** 10mm lepidolite puffy squares
* **21** 10mm x 14mm dyed faceted pink quartz ovals
* **42** 4mm x 6mm Pacific opal Swarovski donuts
* **42** 9mm x 7mm striated blue/green Czech glass ovals
* **42** 6mm sage flat center-drilled Swarovski squares
* **84** 9mm x 7mm lavender Czech glass ovals
* **42** lavender faceted Czech glass donuts
* **1** 3-row cha-cha/expansion bracelet
* **168** silver-plated head pins (you need the strength of silver-plated here)

TOOLS
* round-nose pliers
* snipe-nose pliers
* oblique or flush cutters

RESOURCES: CRYSTAL FROM SWAROVSKI; CZECH GLASS FROM YORK NOVELTY; LEPIDOLITE FROM GREAT CRAFT WORKS; FACETED OVALS FROM PHOENIX JEWELRY AND PARTS; HEAD PINS AND CHA-CHA BRACELET FROM RINGS AND THINGS

BEAD HEAD PINS AND BEGIN ATTACHING TO EXPANDER

BEAD ALL OF YOUR HEAD PINS FIRST OR BEAD THEM AS YOU GO, FOL-
LOWING THE DIAGRAM. TURN A LOOP IN THE HEAD PIN WIRE ABOVE
EACH BEAD. TO BEGIN BEADING THE BRACELET, ATTACH A PINK BEADED
HEAD PIN ("B" IN THE DIAGRAM) TO THE CENTER EXPANDER LINK ON
ONE OF THE LINKS IN THE BRACELET. TO ATTACH THE HEAD PIN, SIMPLY
USE SNIPE-NOSE PLIERS TO OPEN THE HEAD PIN LOOP, SLIP IT ONTO THE
LINK, AND CLOSE THE LOOP TO SECURE IT.

ATTACH ROW 1 BEADS

CONTINUE TO ATTACH THE BEADED HEAD PINS IN THE
FIRST ROW AS ILLUSTRATED IN THE DIAGRAM.

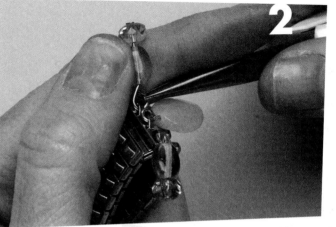

PATIENCE BOOSTER

Tackle this project over the course of
several days, or you may start to feel
overwhelmed. It is the repetition, the
repetition, the repetition that may get to
you. So, don't do it all at once and
save yourself from having an unfinished
cha-cha bracelet sitting in a drawer!

ATTACH ROW 2 BEADS

ATTACH THE BEADED HEAD PINS TO
THE SECOND ROW IN THE PATTERN
AS SHOWN IN THE DIAGRAM. ("E"
AND "A" ARE ATTACHED TO THE
SAME LINK.) REPEAT THE TWO-ROW
PATTERN ALL THE WAY AROUND
THE EXPANDER BRACELET.

ATTACH FINAL
BEADED HEAD PIN

TO ATTACH THE FINAL BEADED HEAD PIN,
HOLD THE BRACELET BENT TIGHTLY DOU-
BLE SO THAT THE REMAINING LINK TO BE
FILLED IS EXPOSED. HOLD THE OTHER
BEADS BACK WITH YOUR FINGERS SO
YOU CAN SEE. SNIPE-NOSE PLIERS REALLY
COME IN HANDY HERE!

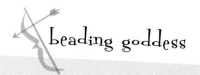
DISCO STAR
NECKLACE

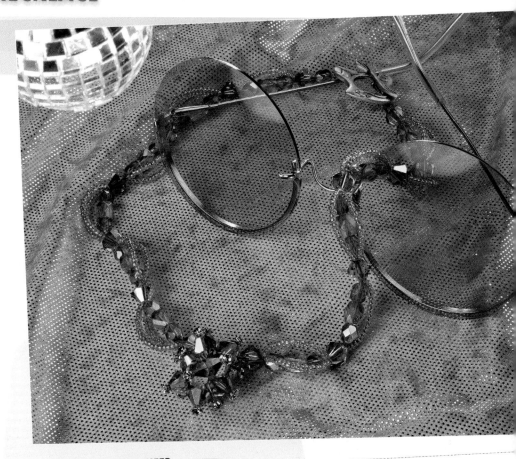

**DRUM ROLL, PLEASE...
HERE IS THE FINAL PROJECT,
A REAL SHOWSTOPPER TO
TEST YOUR BEADING SKILLS
AND YOUR PATIENCE.**
It looks complicated, and it is, but
you are a Bead Queen, so it will
be a piece of cake. Three strands
of beaded wire make a dimensional and curvilinear design...
and the disco star pendant sends
it over the edge. You did it, aren't
you proud of yourself? GO BEAD
QUEEN, GO!!!!!!

WHAT YOU WILL NEED

SUPPLIES (DISCO BALL)
* **14** 8mm light Colorado topaz Swarovski bicones
* **7** black diamond Swarovski chaton head pins
* **7** 8mm crystal Swarovski chaton head pins
* SP eye pin
* 6mm SP jump ring

NECKLACE
* **1** tube size 14 golden yellow seed beads (14 groups of 19)
* **42** 6mm black diamond Czech glass AB faceted rounds
* **14** 8mm light Colorado topaz Swarovski bicones
* **14** 6mm x 8mm grey Czech glass squovals
* frosted free-form Calla lily design toggle clasp
* **2** no. 3 crimp tubes
* **3** 20" (51cm) lengths .013" (.33mm) 49 strand wire

TOOLS
* short snipe-nose pliers
* fine chain-nose pliers
* round-nose pliers
* crimp tool
* oblique or flush cutters

RESOURCES: CRYSTAL FROM SWAROVSKI; CHATON HEAD PINS FROM JEWELRYSUPPLY.COM; TOGGLE CLASP FROM BLUE MOON BEADS; SEED BEADS FROM TOHO; WIRE AND CRIMPS FROM BEADALON

PATIENCE BOOSTER

Create the pendant first and be prepared for some frustration in hooking the beaded head pins onto the eye pin in the center. It may seem to defy the laws of physics once you get to the last few, but it will work…I promise.

CREATE STAR BASE

ATTACH AN EYE PIN TO A JUMP RING. SLIDE ON A LIGHT COLORADO TOPAZ SWAROVSKI BICONE AND CUT THE EYE PIN WIRE DOWN TO ABOUT ⅛" (3MM) ABOVE THE BEAD. MAKE A LOOP IN THE WIRE WITH THE ROUND-NOSE PLIERS.

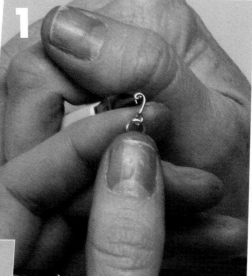

CREATE STAR COMPONENTS AND BEGIN TO BUILD STAR

SLIDE HALF OF THE BICONE CRYSTALS ONTO BLACK CHATONS AND HALF ONTO CRYSTAL CHATONS. CUT THE CHATON WIRE TO ABOUT ⅛" (3MM) ABOVE THE CRYSTALS AND LOOP THE WIRE WITH ROUND-NOSE PLIERS. ATTACH A JUMP RING TO THE EYE PIN LOOP YOU MADE IN STEP ONE THAT YOU WILL BE ABLE TO GRIP AS YOU CONSTRUCT THE STAR. USE VERY FINE CHAIN-NOSE PLIERS TO ATTACH THE FIRST WIRED CRYSTAL TO THE EYE PIN LOOP.

CONTINUE BUILDING STAR

CONTINUE TO ATTACH THE BICONE CRYSTALS ONE BY ONE TO THE EYE PIN LOOP, ALTERNATING BETWEEN BLACK AND CRYSTAL CHATONS. CONTINUE ADDING THE BICONES UNTIL YOU'VE BUILT A THREE-DIMENSIONAL "STAR."

FINISH BUILDING STAR

BE CAREFUL AND PATIENT AS YOU ADD IN THE
VERY LAST BICONE BEAD. IT MAY TAKE SOME
TIME TO ATTACH THE LAST BICONE BEAD, BUT
THE SNIPE-NOSE PLIERS SHOULD BE ABLE TO
REACH INTO THE TIGHT SPACE.

BEGIN STRINGING BEADS

ATTACH THREE 20" (51CM) STRANDS OF WIRE TO A CLASP USING A CRIMP TUBE.
FLATTEN THE CRIMP TUBE WITH THE CRIMPING TOOL. THREAD THE FIRST TWO BEADS,
A 6MM BLACK DIAMOND AB ROUND AND A COLORADO 6MM BICONE, ONTO ALL
THREE STRANDS. THEN THREAD A BLACK DIAMOND ROUND, A 6MM GREY SQUOVAL
AND ANOTHER BLACK DIAMOND ROUND ONTO THE CENTER, OR CORE, STRAND
OF WIRE. THEN THREAD 19 GOLD SEED BEADS ONTO EACH OF THE OUTER TWO
STRANDS. SLIDE ALL THREE STRANDS THROUGH A COLORADO 6MM BICONE BEAD.

CREATE SEED BEAD ARCS

PULL THE WIRE STRANDS TAUT SO THAT THE GOLD SEED
BEADS FORM TWO ARCS.

STRING ON SECOND BEADED SEGMENT

STRING THE NEXT THREE BEADS ONTO THE CORE
WIRE AS IN STEP SIX: BLACK DIAMOND, SQUOVAL,
BLACK DIAMOND. STRING 19 GOLD SEED BEADS
ONTO THE TWO REMAINING STRANDS AND FEED
ALL THREE STRANDS THROUGH A COLORADO
BICONE CRYSTAL.

CONTINUE BEADING IN PATTERN

PULL THE STRANDS TIGHT TO CREATE THE SEED BEAD ARCS. KEEP GOING THROUGH AND ADJUSTING THE WIRES AS YOU GO ALONG. MAINTAINING PROPER TENSION THROUGHOUT THE NECKLACE WILL ALLOW YOU TO FINISH THE NECKLACE MORE EASILY.

DESIGNER TIP

Take this technique to new heights by changing up your core beads...add in more strands for an even funkier effect...hey...you are the bead queen now so I don't need to tell you this stuff anymore...do I?!

ATTACH CLASP

WHEN YOU REACH THE CENTER (JUST AFTER THE SIXTH BEADED SEGMENT), STRING ON A COLORADO TOPAZ 8MM BICONE, TWO 6MM BLACK DIAMOND AB BEADS AND ANOTHER 8MM COLORADO TOPAZ BICONE BEAD. YOU WILL INSERT THE DISCO STAR BETWEEN THE TWO BLACK ROUNDS. CONTINUE BEADING IN THE ESTABLISHED PATTERN UNTIL YOU HAVE USED ALL OF THE BEADS. ATTACH THE OTHER HALF OF THE TOGGLE CLASP USING A CRIMP TUBE AND FLATTEN IT WITH THE CRIMP TOOL.

ATTACH STAR PENDANT

OPEN THE STAR JUMP RING WITH PLIERS AND SLIP IT INTO THE CENTER OF YOUR NECKLACE BETWEEN THE TWO CENTER BLACK DIAMOND AB ROUNDS. SECURE IT TIGHTLY CLOSED WITH YOUR PLIERS.

resources
resources

MOST OF THE SUPPLIES USED TO MAKE THE PROJECTS IN THIS BOOK CAN BE FOUND IN YOUR LOCAL CRAFT, HOBBY, BEAD OR DISCOUNT DEPARTMENT STORES. IF YOU HAVE TROUBLE LOCATING A SPECIFIC PRODUCT, CONTACT ONE OF THE SUPPLY SOURCES LISTED BELOW TO FIND A LOCAL OR INTERNET VENDOR, OR TO REQUEST A CATALOG.

BEADALON
205 Carter Drive
West Chester, PA 19382
www.beadalon.com
866.4-BEADALON
manufacturer and wholesaler of beading wire, stringing materials, findings, tools, Toho seed beads, Paula Radke beads, gemstone and glass beads

THE BEADIN' PATH
15 Main Street
Freeport, ME 04032
www.beadinpath.com
877.92.BEADS
retail vintage Lucite and other unique beads and findings

BLUE MOON BEADS/ WESTRIM CRAFTS
7855 Hayvenhust Avenue
Van Nuys, CA 91406
www.bluemoonbeads.com
800.377.6715
wholesale beads and findings

THE COLOR WHEEL COMPANY
P.O. Box 130
Philomath, OR
www.colorwheelco.com
info@colorwheelco.com
541.929.7526 phone
manufacturer of color wheels

CRYSTAL INNOVATIONS/PURE ALLURE, INC.
4005 Avenida De La Plata
Oceanside, CA 92056
www.pureallure.com
800.536.6312
manufacturer and wholesaler of crystal and metal sliders, clasps, Swarovski crystal beads

EURO TOOL, INC.
14101 Botts Road
Grandview, MO 64030
www.eurotool.com
800.552.3131
wholesale distributor of tools and beading accessories

FIRE MOUNTAIN GEMS AND BEADS
1 Fire Mountain Way
Grants Pass, OR 97526
www.firemountaingems.com
800.355.2137
retailer of beads, findings, tools, stringing materials, kits

GREAT CRAFT WORKS
133 West Gay Street
West Chester, PA 19380
www.greatcraftworks.com
888.811.5773
retailer of beads, tools, stringing materials

HALCRAFT BEAD HEAVEN
60 South Macqueston Parkway
Mount Vernon, NY 10550
www.halcraft.com
212.376.1580
bead and craft manufacturers

HIRSCHBERG SCHUTZ AND CO.
650 Liberty Avenue
Union, NJ 07083
908.810.1111
manufacturer of charms and embellishments

LINDSTROM TOOLS
Top Tier Tools for this book
supplied courtesy of:
Lindstrom Precision Tools
1440 West Taft Avenue
Orange, CA 92865
www.lindstromtools.com
714.921.9950
beading tools manufacturer

MARVIN SCHWAB, THE BEAD WAREHOUSE
2740 Garfield Avenue
Silver Spring, MD 20910
301.565.0487
www.thebeadwarehouse.com
wholesale and retail beads, gems, precious metal findings, stringing materials, tools

NATURAL TOUCH
P.O. Box 2713
Petaluma, CA 94953
www.naturaltouchbeads.com
707.781.0808
importer, wholesaler and retailer of Indonesian resin beads

OFFRAY RIBBON
Berwick Offray LLC
Bomboy Lane and Ninth Street
Berwick, PA 18603
www.offray.com
1.800.BERWICK
ribbon manufacturers

PHOENIX BEADS, JEWELRY AND PARTS
5 West 37th Street
New York, NY 10018
www.phoenixbeads.com
212.278.8688
wholesale gemstone, glass, pearl and crystal beads from around the world

PAULA RADKE DICHROIC GLASS
P.O. Box 1088
Morro Bay, CA 93442
www.paularadke.com
800.341.4945
dichroic glass beads manufacturer

RINGS AND THINGS
PO Box 450
Spokane, WA 99210-0450
www.rings-things.com
800.366.2156
wholesale beads, tools, findings and stringing materials

SWAROVSKI NORTH AMERICA LIMITED
1 Kenney Drive
Cranston, RI 02920-4468
800.463.0849
Swarovski crystal beads and components manufacturer

THUNDERBIRD SUPPLY
1907 West Historic Route 66
Gallup, NM 87301
2311 Vassar NE
Albuquerque, NM 87107
www.thunderbirdsupply.com
800.545.7968
retail beads, findings, gemstones, tools and stringing materials

YORK NOVELTY
10 West 37th Street
New York, NY 10018
www.yorkbeads.com
800.223.6676
wholesale Czech glass beads

index

CHECK OUT OTHER
NORTH LIGHT BOOKS
FOR MORE SASSY *crafting ideas!*

RETRO MANIA
by Judi Watanabe, Alison Eads & Laurie Dewberry
Retro Mania! shows you how to make swell paper-crafts using hot images and graphics from your favorite decades. You'll find 60 projects featuring popular decade-inspired motifs, from the swellegant 40s and fabulous 50s to the psychedelic 60s and groovy 70s. You'll love the stylish handmade cards, scrapbook pages and gift ideas. The book also includes tips on customizing every project to your personal swingin' taste.

ISBN-13 978-1-58180-746-2
ISBN-10 1-58180-746-5, PAPERBACK, 96 PAGES, 33418

BEAD ON A WIRE
by Sharilyn Miller
In her latest book, magazine editor and popular author Sharilyn Miller shows crafters of all levels how to get in on the popularity of jewelry and beading. Inside *Bead on a Wire*, you'll find an in-depth section on design and construction techniques that make it a snap to get started. You'll love to make the 20 step-by-step bead and wire jewelry projects, including gorgeous earrings, necklaces, brooches and bracelets. You'll be amazed at how easy it is to start making fashionable jewelry that's guaranteed to inspire compliments.

ISBN-13 978-1-58180-650-2
ISBN-10 1-58180-650-7, PAPERBACK, 128 PAGES, 33239

SIMPLY BEAUTIFUL BEADING
by Heidi Boyd
Beads give a sense of glamour and fun to everything—jewelry, fabrics and home décor. Author Heidi Boyd will inspire you with over 50 affordable and fashionable projects, including necklaces and bracelets, picture frames, journals and more. Beginners will learn basic beading and jewelry-making techniques, all of which are quick and easy. This book is part of the Simply Beautiful series, which features a simple yet sophisticated approach to popular crafts.

ISBN-13 978-1-58180-563-5
ISBN-10 1-58180-563-2, PAPERBACK, 128 PAGES, 33018

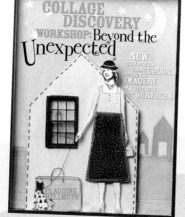

COLLAGE DISCOVERY WORKSHOP: BEYOND THE UNEXPECTED
by Claudine Hellmuth
In her second workshop book, Claudine Hellmuth taps into a whole new level of creativity in *Beyond the Unexpected*. Inside you'll find original artwork and inventive ideas that show you how to personalize your own collage pieces using new techniques and interesting surfaces. In addition, the extensive gallery compiled by Claudine and other top collage artists will spark your imagination. Whether you're a beginner or a collage veteran, you'll enjoy this lovely book both as inspiration and as a practical guide.

ISBN-13 978-1-58180-535-2
ISBN-10 1-58180-535-7, PAPERBACK, 128 PAGES, 33267

THESE AND OTHER FINE NORTH LIGHT TITLES ARE AVAILABLE FROM YOUR LOCAL ART AND CRAFT RETAILER, BOOKSTORE OR ONLINE SUPPLIER.